60
PEOPLE
to Avoid at the
Water Cooler

also by Josh Aiello

A Field Guide to the Urban Hipster

60
PEOPLE
to Avoid at the
Water Cooler

Josh Aiello

with illustrations by Matthew Shultz

Broadway Books   New York

Broadway Books titles may be purchased for business or promotional use or
for special sales. For information, please write to: Special Markets Department, Random House, Inc., 1745 Broadway, New York, NY 10019.

PRINTED IN THE UNITED STATES OF AMERICA

BROADWAY BOOKS and its logo, a letter B bisected on the diagonal, are
trademarks of Random House, Inc.

Visit our website at www.broadwaybooks.com

First edition published 2004

Book design by Laurie Jewell
Illustrated by Matthew Shultz

Library of Congress Cataloging-in-Publication Data
Aiello, Josh.
    60 people to avoid at the water cooler / by Josh Aiello, with illustrations
by Matthew Shultz.— 1st ed.
        p.   cm.
    1. Work—Humor.   2. Human behavior—Humor.   I. Title: Sixty people
to avoid at the water cooler.   II. Title.
PN6231.W644A43 2004
818'.602—dc22   2004043787

ISBN 0-7679-1842-8

10   9   8   7   6   5   4   3   2   1

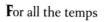For all the temps

CONTENTS

INTRODUCTION

Like death, taxes, and my expanding waistline, office work is an unfortunate fact of life. It can be a degrading and soul-deadening way to earn a living, yet it remains slightly more appealing than, say, selling your body in Atlantic City or working the fryer at McDonald's. At least there's free Internet access, a high-tech coffee machine, and all the Post-its you can swipe from the supply closet. But for the most part it's just awful: more painful than being dumped or rooting for the Philadelphia Phillies. Is the ability to afford food and shelter really worth wasting your life in a cubicle? Apparently so.

If there's anything worse than working in an office, it's temping in one. Trust me—I've spent much of the past six years toiling for an endless sequence of interchangeable corporate masters, yearning for health insurance and awkwardly fumbling about with Microsoft Excel. A few highlights from my fake career: I have been asked (repeatedly) to please stop reading magazines at my desk. I have answered the telephone for a man with half my IQ. I have feigned interest in the rebounding economies of the former Soviet region. I have drained all evidence of Irish slang from a seventy-five-page report on a proposed South American oil pipeline written by an engineer named O'Grady. I have witnessed a woman drunkenly throw up all over herself at a company picnic, then get fired the next morning. I have petitioned HR (unsuccessfully, as it turned out) for the right to work forty straight hours, then take the rest of the week off. I have been referred to, on several occasions, as "one of the girls."

Speaking of HR, I once spent three weeks supposedly assisting with the implementation of a new database intended to facilitate quicker access to employee records. Since this task constituted the most boring experience this side of listening to new parents describe their baby, I mostly amused myself by poring over the sordid details of the staff's year-end reviews. Let's just say a few choice selections made their way into the inner confines of my incredibly stylish messenger bag. These you will find reprinted herein, though I have changed the names to protect the incompetent (and avoid a lawsuit).

In addition to this comedic windfall, I managed to pass the majority of my time obsessing over the pathetic comings and goings of my coworkers and superiors, all the while plotting the glorious day I'd exact my revenge by writing a scathing tell-all on office life. (Cue diabolical laughter.) It didn't take long to notice that, whether I was answering the telephone at Au Bon Pain's corporate headquarters or staring out the window at Bank Boston, each office was populated by the same terrible people, the most preposterous (and common) of which are immortalized here, along with helpful illustrations (for better slacking off). I trust you'll recognize them from your nightmares and company picnics.

60
PEOPLE
to Avoid at the
Water Cooler

Well, well, well. Who's the fresh-faced, perky new hire with the shiny sports car? Perhaps it's the new Consultant or the junior executive with an MBA management has been so eager to find. He certainly seems confident, what with his brisk walk and mastery of the silent head nod greeting technique (used only on those obviously at the bottom of the corporate ladder). And the way he dresses: in the style of Regis Philbin circa *Who Wants to Be a Millionaire?* Only hotshots can pull off that solid-tie-on-solid-shirt look. Seems like you've got one more person to take orders from.

But wait. What's this? He's being shuttled to the smallest cube in the office. He's been given the oldest, slowest computer. You can't even print from that workstation! As long as you've been with the company, only Interns and the occasional brain-dead Temp have been placed under this guy's new supervisor. What gives?

The Alpha Chimp is on the scene. Fresh off his senior year of college, he's now old enough to drink beer at happy hour and is gunning to take control of the company. Stay out of his way if you don't want to get run over in the corridor. The Alpha Chimp is always on the prowl, pseudoimportant documents in hand, trying his damnedest to bump into a major player and score a little face time. He sucks up to the boss with such vigor and regularity that it's possible to pick up a vacuumlike sound if you lower the volume on your headphones. And the ass-kissing! This guy smooches heinie like Joe Montana threw footballs (which is to say: very well).

The Alpha Chimp is the only person in the office who actually admires the Yes Men. Oh, if he could only be one of them! The thought of lunching with the boss is enough to make the Alpha Chimp's heart quiver. With the possible exception of the Hawaiian girl from his freshman Spanish elective, nothing has ever excited the Alpha Chimp quite like the prospect of being counted among the boss's most valued cronies. He spends the majority of his time studying their every move and is already deft with corporate catchphrases. It's virtually impossible to communicate with the Alpha Chimp without being bombarded with several choice turns of phrase picked up in Salesmanship 101: "right-sizing," "win-win," and "out of the box" are among his greatest bits. No matter that these phrases are practically meaningless; they do lend the Alpha Chimp a certain air of superiority as he runs off that stack of copies you requested.

Though a fan of the Yes Men, the Alpha Chimp fears hitting the glass ceiling the way they have. Sure, he's prepared to spend a few years orbiting the boss, but he's got his eyes on the real prize, the head honcho position itself. Start filing his executive washroom key now. The Alpha Chimp begins to separate himself from those around him from day one. He sprinkles patronizing compliments, such as "You're doing a great job—keep up the good work," on coworkers on his level while simultaneously ingratiating himself to the higher-ups by taking up golf, a sport he neither enjoys or excels at. The Alpha Chimp's goal in life is to race up the corporate ladder as quickly as possible. He's after power, money, recognition, and (how to delicately put this?) a semblance of virility. There's a reason certain coworkers refer to the red Trans-Am in the parking lot as the Alpha Chimp's "penis substitute."

In order to advance, the Alpha Chimp must perform well on the job, so he trains for his yearly review as if it's the Olympic Games. A single poor mark can relegate him to another full year in administrative hell. Therefore, he identifies his goals and maps a course for meeting them. The Alpha Chimp spends more time and energy plotting his career path than he does performing any actual work.

The Alpha Chimp's presence in your office can double as a fairly accurate gauge of how old/bitter/jaded/sour/uncommitted you have become, as his fresh-faced enthusiasm offers stark contrast to your own indelible misery. You can practically feel your intestines tightening as the Alpha Chimp, during his second week on the job, throws a birthday party for a certain key member of upper management. It's not long before you, and those like you, begin referring to the Alpha Chimp only as "TLF," or "That Little F***er."

MEMORABLE QUOTES

◆ [To fellow Admin] "What we really need to do is think outside the box [makes square shape with forefingers for emphasis] and deliver more than what the client expects. It's a win-win situation."

◆ "Why don't you go ahead and file those? Oh, right. That's my job."

◆ "[Insert boss's name here] smells wonderful today, doesn't he?"

THE BIG FISH IN A SMALL POND

Though pushing forty, the Big Fish considers himself impervious to the aging process. He is the resident adrenaline junkie and, salt-and-pepper hair notwithstanding, his tastes in clothing, music, automobiles, hobbies, and slang are identical to that of your average college sophomore. He voted for Nader and considers the word "X-Treme" to be a useful adjective. This is the guy who makes you feel old for acting your age. He's also the coworker who most likes to get "in your face."

The presence of a Small Pond is vital to the Fish's classification as Big. Thus, the Big Fish is found only in small, somewhat out-of-the-way, yet still urban environments such as Providence, Rhode Island. Since he lacks any truly exceptional qualities, the Big Fish's illusion of superiority requires the contrast of his simple surroundings. To this end, he never makes the leap to larger, more competitive environments (such as New York or even Boston) even though the opportunity occasionally presents itself. He enjoys and excels at aiming low.

Admittedly, the Big Fish does maintain an admirable physical condition, especially for a man his age. He is a strict adherent to fad diets such as Atkins and regularly works out. In order to flaunt his health-conscious lifestyle, he exercises only on his lunch break (returning to the office still perspiring) before ostentatiously devouring either a salad or grilled chicken breast at his desk. He is also quite dapper and refuses to participate in any event requiring him to dress down (like casual Friday). However, the Big Fish will jump at any opportunity (perhaps an interoffice volleyball game) to show off his favorite obnoxious sunglasses (always mirrored, sometimes tinted). For such events, he will change into superstylish, freshly pressed athletic gear.

The Big Fish situates himself in an exterior, preferably two-sided cubicle. Once ensconced, he is afforded a pristine view of the office proper and is able to keep track of all social developments. The Big Fish is a master of cubicle decoration. He possesses a certain artistry and understands precisely which objects will trigger what reaction. Common installations include photographs of himself skydiving (athleticism and daring), foreign objets d'art (globe-trotting), posted football pool results (hey, he's just one of the guys), hardbound texts pertaining to his professional area of expertise (competence), and one pedestrian classic along the lines of *The Iliad* or *The Divine Comedy* (literacy and intelligence). Furthermore, and most preposterously, he often tries to appear sophisticated by creating what he regards as keenly literate scrolling screensaver texts (*"Après moi, le déluge,"* for example). Snarky coworkers have been known to reply with parody screensavers of their own (*"Veni, vidi, vici"*). The Big Fish doesn't get the joke.

In some ways similar to the Water Cooler Casanova, the Big Fish in a Small Pond does not share the former's unquenchable sexual appetite. Of course, the Big Fish also finds the Office Girls enchanting, but he is too concerned with strutting about like a well-endowed peacock to get bogged down in any potentially emotional predicament. He flirts a little and can get a bit rowdy at happy hour, but ultimately the Big Fish would rather work on his delts than cheat on his wife. Still, the two are good friends, and often play golf or watch *TRL* together after work.

MEMORABLE QUOTES

◆ "Do you snowboard?"

◆ "Let's get a few Michelob Ultras after work."

◆ [Upon allowing a coworker to borrow a few CDs from his extensive collection of underground, esoteric artists] "Go ahead, expand your mind."

◆ "I know every bouncer in Hartford."

Employee: The Brown Noser

> **Only the most significant and important points need to be recorded as a reference for the next review.**

The Brown Noser will stop at nothing to get ahead—well, except for resorting to hard work. Basically a Yes Man of lower station, the Brown Noser suppresses her own opinions as effectively as a 1950s housewife, yet must make do kissing the asses of mid-level management, as she has no real access to the Pompous General Partner himself (yet).

The Brown Noser's lack of pride may be the residual result of having suffered some long suppressed social catastrophe, such as being stood up at the prom or compared aesthetically to the family pooch. As it is, most coworkers marvel over her nonstop fawning and treacly appreciation for all aspects of her superior's business acumen, fashion sense, social life, and politics. The Brown Noser is incapable of disagreement and will even swear allegiance to moves and policies destined to work out badly for her and her coworkers in the long run. She will coo over any baby picture ("Ooh, pudgy babies are just the cutest!"), alter her position on any subject at a moment's notice ("Did I say 'pro-choice'? Huh. Well, I meant 'pro-life'"), and stroke the egos of all who will listen ("It's amazing how well you file.").

The Brown Noser is impervious to mistreatment and apparently cannot recognize when she is being taken advantage of. In addition to sucking up, the Brown Noser jumps at any opportunity to stab a coworker in the back if it will benefit her own career. She has been known to tattle, fib, and tell tales out of school all during the course of a single afternoon. The Brown Noser has no real friends and has recently stooped to trolling for dates online.

Comments and Recommendations: Flattery should get her everywhere.

PERFORMANCE REVIEW AND DEVELOPMENT REPORT

Employee: The Caffeine Junkie

> **Only the most significant and important points need to be recorded as a reference for the next review.**

The Caffeine Junkie averages roughly three and a half minutes of work per mug of coffee. He is always in motion, a condition that manifests itself both in the form of a continuous desk–kitchen–men's room loop and an intense series of jittery twitching primarily affecting his hands, feet, and head. While at his desk, the Caffeine Junkie must either fiddle with a pencil, tap his legs in rhythm to some unheard, up-tempo arrangement, or shift back and forth until he has worn through the seat of his trousers.

He has a crazed countenance that grows maniacal in the event that a coworker beats him to the coffeemaker. The Caffeine Junkie is incapable of hiding his contempt for interlopers who fumble with his favorite apparatus like clumsy jocks trying to unhook their first bra. The Caffeine Junkie has no time for such trifles as milk or sugar, though he will occasionally deign to shake some nondairy creamer into his favorite mug, a once white ceramic number now stained a light brown. He will sometimes mix things up on his lunch hour by patronizing the nearest Dunkin' Donuts drive-through, but before doing so fills a mug for the road.

The Caffeine Junkie has far and away the worst breath in the office, a situation compounded by his preference for speaking to coworkers from a maximum distance of six inches. He gets along fairly well with other employees, excepting the equally caffeine-loving Potential Serial Killer, to whom the Caffeine Junkie usually (and wisely) opts to cede common ground for reasons of safety. In a pinch, the Caffeine Junkie will resort to Mountain Dew or even chocolate, though such stopgaps rarely satiate him for long. His productivity wanes significantly with each attempt to give up caffeine, thus persuading him to forego good health for performance. He is a valued employee, though a bit hard to stomach at times.

Comments and Recommendations: Impending heart attack should limit his chances for promotion.

9

PERFORMANCE REVIEW AND DEVELOPMENT REPORT

Employee: The Cheapskate

> **Only the most significant and important points need to be recorded as a reference for the next review.**

It seems a bunch of the Cheapskate's coworkers are pooling their resources in order to procure Chinese food for lunch. The Cheapskate likes the sound of that. He could really go for some chicken lo mein. The Cheapskate voices his agreement and places his order. He then returns to work, practically salivating at the thought of his impending Oriental feast. The Cheapskate is the first one at the food bag, greedily removing his own dishes from the parcel before disappearing to parts of the office unknown.

He eats in seclusion, preferring a magazine's company to that of his coworkers. Whoever placed the order and collected the money for it is stuck looking for the Cheapskate all afternoon with the tab for his meal. He isn't seen again until several days later, whereupon all memory of his free lunch has faded. If, on the rare chance that a coworker mentions it, the Cheapskate performs an intricate dance of patted pockets, opened wallet (tilted so that all may see its emptiness), and turned-over pencil mug, designed to display the severe nature of his poverty.

He is savvy enough not to take advantage of those around him too often, and therefore manages to score free lunches, coffee, snacks, and office supplies on a semiregular basis. When he suspects his days of successful swindling may be numbered, the Cheapskate orchestrates some ostentatious display of his own generosity, such as springing for pizza for the entire office (but only on two-for-one day). In doing so, he is able to purchase enough goodwill to allow him to take advantage of his coworkers for another six months or so.

Comments and Recommendations: His monetary ingenuity could lead to a nice career in accounting or finance.

PERFORMANCE REVIEW AND DEVELOPMENT REPORT

Employee: The Chitchat Artist

> **Only the most significant and important points need to be recorded as a reference for the next review.**

The Chitchat Artist ruminates on only the most drearily obvious and uninteresting subjects, such as the weather, the days of the week, or his latest weekend plans (which most likely involve some unbelievably boring account of his efforts to redo the upstairs bathroom). No matter where they are or how pressing their business at hand, coworkers seem to encounter the Chitchat Artist at every turn. He displays a knack for "swinging by" (his term) the office or cubicle of whoever happens to be busiest and least interested in conversation.

His professional function is a complete mystery to all, save perhaps his immediate supervisor. No one knows where his desk is, or if he even has one. The Chitchat Artist prefers to spend the majority of his day either riding the elevator or standing at the urinal. He will typically instigate contact by either a nod of the head or a complicit rolling of the eyes, physical actions quickly followed by several favorite stock phrases calling for no response, such as "Hump Day . . . we're halfway there" or "(sigh) . . . What a grind."

Recipients/victims usually greet these statements with some variation on the word "yeah," often coupled with an optional single click of the tongue. Such coworkers then find themselves stuck on the quiet end of a fifteen-minute "conversation," the details of which are completely lost to them immediately thereafter. The Chitchat Artist is incapable of noticing that a coworker happens to be on the telephone, and thinks nothing of proceeding with his personal take on the morning's rainstorm regardless.

Comments and Recommendations: Lack of actual output and his ability to annoy even the most patient of supervisors makes the prospect of promotion (or even continued employment) highly unlikely.

THE COLLEGE INTERN

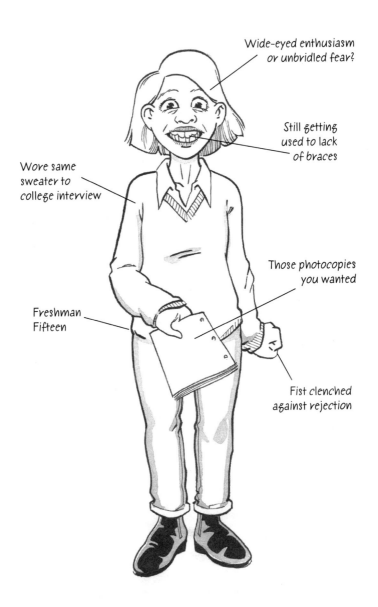

Wide-eyed enthusiasm or unbridled fear?

Still getting used to lack of braces

Wore same sweater to college interview

Those photocopies you wanted

Freshman Fifteen

Fist clenched against rejection

Despite the Emancipation Proclamation's having been ratified in 1863, the College Intern slogs through her workday with chattel-like determination and is compensated only with token rewards of questionable value, such as "experience" and "college credit." How exactly fetching your morning bagel constitutes an educational experience is anybody's guess, yet the College Intern is happy to oblige. But she'd better not forget the cream cheese or she can kiss that recommendation goodbye.

While most normal college students spend their summer breaks backpacking through Europe, lifeguarding at hometown lakes, or retaking the freshman English requirement they slept through during spring term, the College Intern busies herself getting a head start on her professional career. Rising at dawn to commute in from Mom and Dad's house, she's a real go-getter. Of course, her spirit and will to live should be crushed by mid-August, but initially her perkiness will result in an efficiency of envelope-stuffing the likes of which you've never seen. Take advantage of her while you can.

In her rotating repertoire of five brand-new work outfits (or, as her assignment progresses, an Old Navy-issued jeans and sweater combo), the College Intern is overly enthusiastic, yet often thoroughly incompetent. She is idealistic to the point of annoyance, so completely draining her spirit will take some time. But what better place for it than your office? Despite the College Intern's desire to excel, she is often terrified of the regular employees and lives in constant fear of disturbing their work. Expect heavy doses of confused stuttering and stammering. Of course, this doesn't stop her from haranguing her supervisors with the incessant query "What should I do next?" Managing the College Intern is a bit like babysitting the main character from *Memento* and can be a real hassle for people trying to slack off for a few hours. Regardless of this willingness to please, she will do anything within her power to avoid contact of any kind with the office's IT staff, who intimidate the hell out of her. The College Intern will continue to use a keyboard with no space bar if it means not talking to the computer guy.

When not being worked like a field hand, the College Intern spends most of her time in one of two ways: obsessively checking her college Web site or attempting to fend off the Water Cooler Casanova's advances (cute, female Interns only). She speaks of college ad nauseam and, if an Ivy Leaguer, drops the name of her school at least twice a day in case you've forgotten. Despite her most determined efforts, she will wind up drunk and in the Casanova's clutches before summer is out.

As you are no doubt already aware, the College Intern comes in a variety of shapes and sizes. The most common are listed below:

1. *The Little Princess Intern.* Often found in magazine offices (especially those published by Condé Nast), the Little Princess is able to afford her stylish urban internship (which does not offer course credit) due to Daddy's generous allowance. Her boots are worth more than your yearly salary, and, though only twenty, she regularly frequents nightclubs you've only read about in your magazine's society pages. The Little Princess works Monday through Thursday in order to beat the Friday traffic to her beach house.

2. *The Vaguely Recalled Intern.* Utterly nameless and faceless, coworkers vaguely remember her as being "very nice" or perhaps "pleasant." When pressed for personal detail, the normally deathly quiet Vaguely Recalled Intern will mention a keen interest in the life of her oboe-playing or poetry-writing boyfriend, but little else. She works with her head down and studiously avoids small talk. After her assignment ends, she will forever be referred to as "What was her name?" and former coworkers who run into her on the street will have absolutely no idea where they know her from.

3. *The Unnecessarily Hyper Intern.* Often male, the Unnecessarily Hyper Intern runs for your coffee like Edwin Moses and begs for work like Rickey Henderson. His god-awful pep is thoroughly immune to contamination by your own misery and sadness. The Hyper Intern arrives at the office three hours before you do in order to color coordinate your files and triage your paper clips according to diminishing size. After moving on, he will proceed to flood your inbox with e-mails punctuated with emoticons and smiley faces until you change your address.

Perhaps most rare (and dreaded) is the *College Intern Whose Father Owns the Company*. Needless to say, such Interns are as pompous as they are bored with you and your insignificant position. They shirk all responsibility and show up to "work" half a day at best. Their supervisors are obviously powerless to reprimand them (or, unthinkably, terminate their assignment), though fortunately these Interns generally stop coming in at all halfway through the summer.

MEMORABLE QUOTES

◆ "They were all out of yogurt cream cheese, so I got you veggie instead, 'cause I figured it's good for you since it has vegetables in it. I hope that's OK. I also put skim milk in your coffee, so I guess the two sort of even out, right? What? You wanted the bagel scooped out? . . . um, no, I forgot to ask for that. Let me go back, I'll be fast, OK? OK, I'm really sorry . . . can I get some more money?"

◆ "I'm really sorry to bother you, but . . . is it all right if I go to lunch now?"

◆ "I just assumed you wanted the letter double-spaced. That's how my English professor does it."

◆ "Standard margins?"

THE CONDESCENDING IT GUY

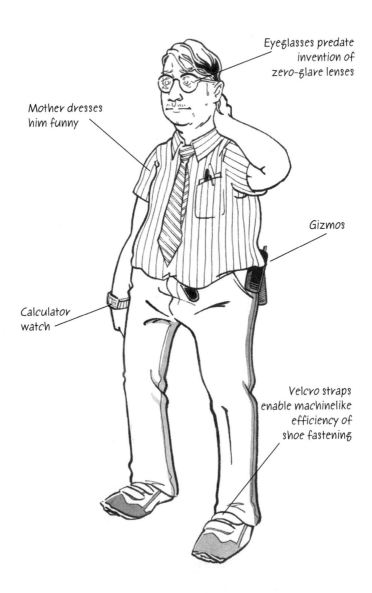

Eyeglasses predate invention of zero-glare lenses

Mother dresses him funny

Gizmos

Calculator watch

Velcro straps enable machinelike efficiency of shoe fastening

The Condescending IT Guy knows all the angles. He has managed to pull the wool over management's eyes and has even ingratiated himself with the Pompous General Partner. By hypnotizing his superiors with a gargled spell of techie low English, the Condescending IT Guy avoids all participation in office protocol and etiquette. He need not engage in conversation or civility and considers it unnecessary to respond to most inquiries. The Condescending IT Guy can say or do anything without fear of reprisal. Apparently, the ability to fix a computer doubles as a moral get-out-of-jail-free card. Certain CITGs have even been known to woo women through secret access to company mailboxes (victims report invitations to dinner and Community College Christmas parties), a dating technique that would no doubt result in both rejection and sexual harassment charges for the rest of you.

Often referred to as "Tech Support" (and officially a "Network Administrator"), the Condescending IT Guy is a walking workplace hazard by any name. Though most office workers try to avoid him like the plague (or overtime), the fact that practically all modern business is computerized guarantees a morphine-like reliance on the CITG. He is frantically summoned to address each digitized hiccup, though his strange ability to be out of the office or otherwise unavailable at the exact moment your computer is "totally freaking out" can result in a lag time only slightly less unbearable than the period between submitting an expense report and receiving compensation.

The real fun begins once the Condescending IT Guy finally deigns to pay a professional visit to your workstation. Self-important in the extreme, he will begin by ignoring everything you have to say in favor of haughtily recommending his favorite remedy: the good old-fashioned reboot. Once you've managed to convey that you've already tried this five times to no avail, all communication will quickly break down. As he attends to your problem, he will proceed either to a) shower you with strange and random anecdotes from his personal life (such as the exploits of his three-legged dog) or, more likely, b) bore you with a litany of incredibly complex lingo designed to enlighten you as to the precise reason for the malfunction you are currently experiencing. Either way, the length of this dialogue can be excruciating. After all, you just want him to leave already so you can get back to studying tonight's matchups on ESPN.com. Can't this guy take a hint?

The Condescending IT Guy is perhaps the only person in the office for whom a job well done results in not having to do any more work. In other words, if all the computers are running smoothly, he's free to just sit around and speculate as to the possibility of an unexpected fourth *Lord of the Rings* installment. In this one respect, the CITG is regarded as a genius by his coworkers, whose own industriousness is rewarded only with another stack of mindless busywork. The Condescending IT Guy spends the majority of his time in a far-off corner cube (or, if he's lucky, behind the closed door of a small office he's somehow managed to procure) completely caught up in his own little world of technological intrigue. Most reside in a work area resembling the nest of a large bird. Surrounded by piles of paper, clumps of trash, and scattered boxes full of strange electronic doodads, these pack rats barely have enough room on their desks for their daily late-afternoon helpings of soft-serve ice cream (in a dish, of course). When interrupted at his desk, the Condescending IT Guy will look up and blink puzzledly at you like a mole emerging into direct sunlight.

For all their hacker-esque love of technology, Condescending IT Guys are sticklers for rules and regulations. They live in constant, paralyzing fear of electronic viruses and therefore are practically fascist in their determination to thwart you from doing anything cool with your computer. If the Condescending IT Guy happens to notice the existence of, say, Limewire on your hard drive, rest assured that file-sharing protection software will be uploaded to your desktop faster than you can say "I don't even know what Limewire is."

In certain low-paying industries (public health, for example), the typical Condescending IT Guy will possess a degree of computer expertise about on par with that of your average Radio Shack employee. In such offices, the CITG's incompetence may be calculated by applying the formula $x + 7 = y$ to each trip he makes to your cubicle, where x represents the original number of complaints he's come to address and y indicates the number of things he will break while there. Applying some simple calculus shows that there is a threshold after which point your computer will no longer be functional and you will need to request a new one. Eight months after this request is made, a new computer arrives, but of course you are now required to have the same IT Guy come and set it up, since you have absolutely no right to install software on your own.

Though for all intents and purposes social loners, Condescending IT Guys often travel in groups or as a pair while working (cliques are formed based on preferred platform, so Windows guys hang out with other Windows guys, and Mac with Mac). It's hard to say whether or not clusters of IT Guys actually function as "friends" as we generally understand the term, but it should go without saying that the IT lunch table is far and away the creepiest corner of the cafeteria. A setting as devoid of females as it is encumbered with brown bag lunches, their lunch table provides a perfect respite for the Condescending IT Guy, who, safe among his fellow geeks, may ruminate on the delightful fact that, though he isn't actually all that bright or worldly, he's making a lot more money than anyone else in the office.

MEMORABLE QUOTES

◆ "So . . . you want to send a 20 meg file over our T1 Line to plot in California? NFW." ["NFW" = "No freaking way."]

◆ "Did you reboot? [Pause for employee response.] "Oh, I see . . . um, did you reboot?"

◆ IT Guy: "The reason your computer keeps freezing up is that you've downloaded too much music to your hard drive."

Employee: "But that makes no sense. We have firewall restrictions that prevent me from downloading music files. Show me the files on my hard drive."

IT Guy: [Long pause/blank stare.] "Did you try to reboot? How 'bout we try that?"

Employee: The Conniving Administrative Assistant

> **Only the most significant and important points need to be recorded as a reference for the next review.**

The Conniving Administrative Assistant has both ambition and bridges to burn. She professes a maniacal desire to get ahead and finds that equal parts hard work and sabotage seem to offer the greatest chance of success. The Conniving Administrative Assistant excels at creating an illusion of dedicated dependability while simultaneously working to ingratiate herself to those who may one day enable her to leapfrog her boss on the corporate ladder.

Cute but not intimidatingly so, she corners valued clients at after-work gatherings in order to make drunken queries as to the possibility of a future business relationship. The presence of alcohol allows the Conniving Administrative Assistant to claim that she has no memory of such a conversation should the particulars make their way back to her superior. Her sales pitch generally involves the notion that she is much smarter/talented/dedicated than is her boss, though how exactly such concepts are illustrated by her admittedly competent telephone and e-mail skills isn't entirely clear.

Clients caught in her web feel nothing but awkwardness and rarely, if ever, report the situation (or even mention it) to her superior. Most will, however, keep the Conniving Administrative Assistant on their good side on the off chance that she does actually manage to supplant those ahead of her.

It is not her impassioned desire to get ahead that raises red flags but the fact that she will stop at nothing to achieve her goals. In certain scenarios, she will go so far as to disregard both company policy and propriety when such grandstanding may serve to impress significant passersby. Nevertheless, she is quite adept at fetching coffee and triaging callers and is therefore a much relied upon member of the staff.

Comments and Recommendations: Should succeed in pulling the rug out from under her boss at some point before next year's review.

THE CONSULTANTS

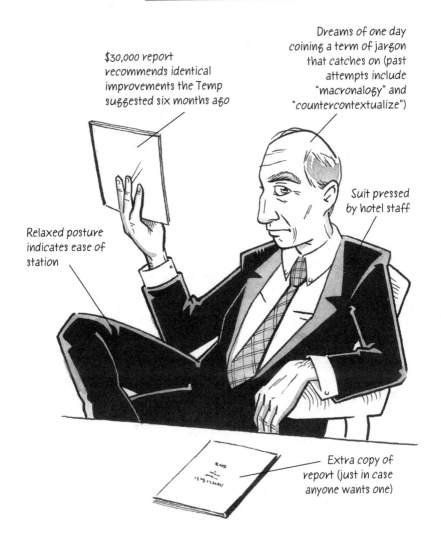

Dreams of one day coining a term of jargon that catches on (past attempts include "macronalogy" and "countercontextualize")

$30,000 report recommends identical improvements the Temp suggested six months ago

Suit pressed by hotel staff

Relaxed posture indicates ease of station

Extra copy of report (just in case anyone wants one)

Let's be honest. No one has any real idea what it is that these people do. Revered by management and loathed by staff (except the Floozy, who's swept away by the money they throw around at happy hour), Consultants aren't Temps or Freelancers exactly, though they are sometimes hired to help the office out of a momentary jam or to temporarily support an overextended workforce. Specific details of their purpose and function can be sketchier than accounts of this year's Christmas bonuses.

Management often hires Consultants to validate ideas it has already formulated. By acquiring the assessment of a third party "independent" source, management feels justified moving forward with whatever mystical initiative they have concocted. Benefits are manifold: First, Consultants perform a task that is somehow unpleasant (like downsizing) or that management is simply too lazy, cowardly, or unqualified to perform itself. Second, Consultants afford management the opportunity to deflect political heat or blame if/when their pet project backfires (at which time management will claim, "We were just following the advice of our Consultants"). And finally, despite their exorbitant hourly fees, Consultants are actually cheaper in the long run than real employees, since they don't receive benefits and no resources are wasted training them. If you've ever glanced at your pay stub, you know how much management likes to cut corners.

There are two main types of Consultants: Management and IT. Management Consultants are called in when the company feels it necessary to perform a little organizational restructuring. These are the Consultants you have every right to fear. They will waltz in, hang out for a few months, examine the company's structure and practices, suggest a few changes (such as firing you), help implement these changes (saving management the trouble), then move on to greener pastures while you file for unemployment.

IT Consultants are both more common and less forbidding. They are summoned to perform some specific technical task that the client company is unqualified to handle in-house. IT Consultants specialize in unbelievably dreary work, such as converting from one database system to another or updating the office's computer servers. Giant nerds and geeks, IT Consultants work for something called "systems integration specialists" and enjoy attending Burning Man in their spare time. Due to their technical expertise, IT Consultants are incredibly expensive and are thus hired for as short a period of time as possible (lucky bastards).

In addition to the preposterous amount of money they rake in, Consultants enjoy more perks than the CEO's mistress, most of which are a direct result of their travel schedules. Consultants are usually assigned to far-flung locations and fly home for the weekends. Thus, their flight schedules double as a handy excuse to stroll in late on Monday and leave by noon on Friday (if they bother to come in at all). Since they are technically always traveling, their expenses are always covered. They take as long a lunch break as they like and even bill for time spent in the air. What's more, Consultants are enrolled in every travel rewards program known to man. They regularly rack up hundreds of thousands of points on hotels, rental cars, and frequent-flier miles for business travel paid for by the client. Let's just say that their oft-neglected girlfriends can look forward to a nice free trip to Italy next summer.

Consultants are sometimes scoffed at for having different-colored ID badges than everyone else and for foolishly wearing a suit on Company Luau Day. Some are recently minted MBAs who couldn't find a real job after graduating. Most are never whisked around for a proper introduction when they start work and are thereafter referred to only as "The Consultant." But these guys have discovered the greatest corporate loophole since you figured out how to steal software off the server. The boss has a better grasp on time travel than on what these guys are doing in his office, thanks mainly to their habit of speaking in jargon indecipherable to the layperson. They are thus free to do basically as they please.

So how does one become a Consultant? Ironically, most are former managers who became Consultants after other Consultants concluded that their positions were unnecessary. Got that? And now they land Consultant gigs thanks to the generosity of executives all too happy to do old colleagues a favor. If you like tons of money and little work, this is the job for you. Salaries are for suckers.

MEMORABLE QUOTES

◆ "The addition of these three graphs into this PowerPoint presentation gives the client the value-added solution they expect from us."

◆ "Sorry, I'm leaving early today."

◆ "We'd appreciate it if you didn't make a scene on your way out the door."

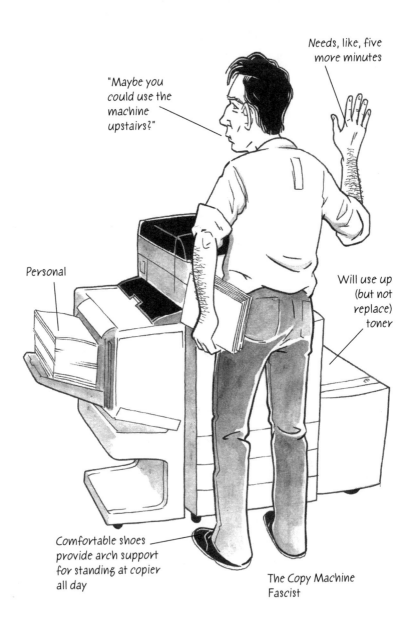

Sure, any idiot (and most members of middle management) can run off a few simple, black-and-white copies, but for those more difficult assignments, the type requiring skill, grace, and the careful collation of double-sided sheets with single, it's best to leave things to the experts. Like other office nether regions (the mailroom and supply closet come to mind), the copy center can be a mysterious, sun-free realm with its own peculiar bylaws and customs. As when conducting an anthropological study, it's best not to tamper with or influence the intricate goings-on of the copy center's inhabitants. Theirs is a culture steeped in paper cuts and toner; they are unfamiliar with your newfangled e-business solutions. Just wait patiently by the door until they have completed your request.

Temps are the office personnel most likely to cross over the threshold of the copy room, though Office Girls have also been known to frequent the location. You've no doubt spent a frantic few moments before the machine, completely befuddled as to how exactly one manages to shrink a copy of the boss's legal-size cell phone bill onto a letter-size expense report. Such are the tasks of which migraines are made and, aside from the all-important work of arranging files in "alpha order," the kind of thing most likely to fill a lower-level Administrative Assistant's schedule. Don't feel too bad, though. The cockpit of the space shuttle is more intuitive than your copier's control panel. This machine makes employees of all ranks weak in the knees and has left better Admins than you crumpled over in tears. The copy room is the office worker's kryptonite; even those of incredible authority (the Pompous General Partner, say) are instantly rendered powerless upon entering the machine's domain.

It's best to avoid the copier altogether, though your boss's frothing mouth and mounting blood pressure can make demurring rather difficult. Fortunately, in many offices regular employees are forbidden, or at least discouraged, from personally handling the copier, and are instead instructed to leave all such tasks to the professionals. The subculture of the copy center is comprised mainly of the following individuals, none of whom should be invited to your next happy hour:

The **Copy Machine Fascist** is merely an interloper, yet one whose official rank makes the act of forcibly removing him from the machine something of an impossibility. The Fascist attempts to use the copier only at the precise instant you've been handed some superpriority one-page photocopying assignment. As you stand there shuffling back and forth or pacing from side to side (while your boss glares a hole through the back of your skull), the Fascist continues to monopolize the office's only photocopier, refusing to budge even for an instant. He will remain at the controls of the photocopier until every last sheet of his immense "priority" project is completed. This can take hours. The Fascist is, of course, encountered only in offices in which the staff does have access to the machine.

The **Copy Machine Maestro** is, despite the title, usually female and the official denizen of the copy room. She actually has a desk beside the machine and can perform feats of photocopying unimaginable to mere mortals. You need that report collated, punched with double staples, shrunk down, bound into a book? She's got you covered. This is a woman who actually makes copies all day and, as a result of her unbelievably stress-free job, is often in a better mood than everyone else. She is sweet and nice and will even sew on a button for you if you lose one. But make no mistake: she is a highly qualified, classically trained technician. In addition to her color-copying prowess, the Maestro can repair almost any jam. She can navigate the machine's intricate maze of slots and compartments and knows precisely which components you shouldn't touch, as they are either quite hot or covered in ink. With the precision of a surgeon, the Maestro is able to extract the tiniest pieces of ripped paper from the machine's innards.

Occasionally, however, a technical problem arises that falls outside the abilities of even the Maestro. Usually caused by a meddling Temp on short assignment, the issue requires professional assistance of a type employed only by the copier manufacturer itself. Thus, the **Copy Machine Doctors,** a uniformed task force incapable of small talk and comprised mainly of techs unable to cut it as network administrators, are summoned. Auto mechanics of the business world, the Copy Machine Doctors work in teams of two or three and are outfitted in one-piece jumpsuits bearing a name over the left breast. It is best to leave them be as their ink-stained fingertips whiz over the deep recesses of the copy machine's interior. Once finished, the Doctors disappear as suddenly as they appeared, leaving you free to break the machine again in another half hour or so.

MEMORABLE QUOTES

◆ "Do NOT leave paper clips lying near the machine! That's exactly how jams happen."

◆ "Every color copy you make costs the company five cents, so be careful."

◆ "Is that screenplay you're copying official business?"

PERFORMANCE REVIEW AND DEVELOPMENT REPORT

Employee: The Courier

> **Only the most significant and important points need to be recorded as a reference for the next review.**

Despite a rabid refusal to dress in business wear and a disposition that actually frightens most people in the office, the Courier is a trustworthy, heavily relied upon delivery person. It remains unclear how myriad facial piercings and enough tattoos to intrigue Diane Arbus allow the Courier to deliver and retrieve packages with a speed unknown to other forms of land travel, but his ability to exceed expectations is as reliable as the firm's insistence on stifling creativity.

The Courier rarely deigns to interact with other workers, save for occasionally prompting them to sign and print their names on the foldout, crumpled-up spreadsheet kept stuffed inside some easy-to-access courier bag pouch or other. He will, however, consent to linger at offices in which attractive female Receptionists handle delivery duties. In such situations, the Courier derives great pleasure from flirtatiously describing his disdain for automobile traffic or regaling the Receptionist with in-depth descriptions of the time he managed to deliver some superimportant marketing report through an unseasonably brutal snowstorm.

Most mysterious is the Courier's willingness to ensure the smooth operation of capitalism while pathetically ranting against the corporate work ethic and scoffing at the mindless office drones whose bidding he nonetheless performs. It seems his desires to pay rent and periodically upgrade the quality of the antitheft device on his bicycle thoroughly trump any political beliefs he claims to hold.

Comments and Recommendations: No viable skills other than ability to ride a bicycle; professional prospects moreover likely to be limited by crippling traffic accident.

PERFORMANCE REVIEW AND DEVELOPMENT REPORT

Employee: The Day Jobber

> **Only the most significant and important points need to be recorded as a reference for the next review.**

Once he consented to turning down the volume of the avant jazz blasting from his computer's speakers, it became possible to catch the Day Jobber actually refer to himself as an "artist" as he readied himself to take dictation from his cantankerous boss across the hall.

Nestled in a windowless, out-of-the-way alcove doubling as a way station for misplaced Hi-Liters, dusty floppy disks, and ancient employee handbooks, the Day Jobber seems strangely attracted to a position he claims is merely "just for now" or "OK until I figure things out." Having recently celebrated his tenth anniversary with the company, the Day Jobber shares a more substantial history with his "day job" than he does with either his wife (the modern dance student) or his longest-running musical "gig" (a jazz combo whose several 5:30 p.m. play dates require the Day Jobber to duck furtively out a half hour early).

He serves as a cautionary tale to coworkers with similar hopes and dreams (such as the Creative Temp), who regard his stagnancy as a signal to, if nothing else, keep moving. Now entering middle age, it seems unlikely that the Day Jobber will ever manage to achieve artistic success or advance past the firm's lower administrative levels.

Comments and Recommendations: Should remain on administrative level for life, barring some unforeseen explosion of public demand for chamber music.

THE DINOSAUR

Biggest influence on hairstyle = Johnny Unitas

Pulsing vein

Eye for detail

Last member of staff to still use a pencil

Years of service, carefully documented and filed for eventual perusal by no one

The Dinosaur regards casual Friday as an affront to his old-school sensibilities. Likewise, he doesn't understand "all this computer crap" (instead, he works most things out by hand, then passes his scribbles over to a subordinate for a little data entry, using his computer only for the calculator feature and occasional letter writing) and tosses off dated conversational slang words (like "ditto") that mean absolutely nothing to his younger assistants. The Dinosaur is out of place and out of touch, but still hanging in there. Lucky for you.

The Dinosaur isn't actually all that old, just outdated. Perhaps sixty-five (at most), he'll be retiring in a few weeks, but until the moment he walks out the door, he will stick to the letter and force his subordinates to perform every last piece of work perfectly. He's particularly keen on attempting to master the new software package that won't be up and running until after he's long gone (not that he'd use it anyway). You'd think a guy might relax a little and enjoy himself, take a load off, coast to the finish line. Not the Dinosaur. He has integrity, damn it, if not a personal interest in actual toil. A meteor would have to crash into the earth to slow his department down. Of course, youth-obsessed upper-management would be happy to arrange such a catastrophe if it were within their power, but instead they just pressure the Dinosaur into accepting a lovely and generous retirement package. They're looking to replace him with someone more dynamic, a bit more forward-thinking. Maybe a little less on the geriatric side.

The Dinosaur is an avowed curmudgeon. He absolutely despises everyone around him, from the Temps straight up to the

CEO. Those in his immediate vicinity must speak in a whisper or risk triggering his temper. He will growl at anyone who asks for a paper clip, and God help you if he overhears you chatting on the telephone. There are few sights more frightening than the specter of the Dinosaur's face rising over the wall of your cubicle. But at least he's consistent. In the same gruff manner that he mistreats his subordinates, he stubbornly refuses to play the games necessary for high promotion. He has no time for golf or ass-kissing or staying late to socialize. He simply can't be bothered. The Dinosaur has a loyal wife at home and a slew of fascinatingly dreadful hobbies that need his attention (repainting the garage, carving small birds out of driftwood).

When the Dinosaur is your supervisor, you'll soon become aware of a startling disparity: his rigid work ethic extends only to your endeavors, not to his. That is, you're the one who'd better do everything just so and keep your downtime to a strict minimum. The Dinosaur is just going to hang out at his desk, studying the Staples catalog (prompting the office wiseass to eventually inquire, "When's the exam?") and bitching about the latest missive sent his way by upper management. If you're looking to be inspired, you've come to the wrong place. The Dinosaur exerts the least amount of energy possible. The most challenging feat he performs is the morning rinse of his dentures (in a glass on his desk). Keep your trap shut and your personality in check. And don't even think of turning that radio on.

In times of crises, however, the Dinosaur will spring into action to defend his troops. In his mind, there is no chance that the department under his command is capable of committing an error or working too slowly. The Dinosaur will go to bat for his assistants more for the chance to clash with management than for any real love for or trust in those around him (generally a loose confederacy of absentminded Temps, perky Office Girls, and beat-upon Sappy Matrons). As soon as the crisis is averted and order restored, he will revert back to his petulant self.

As retirement day grows near, the Dinosaur will suffer visions of his impending purposelessness. He has no plans for retirement and dreads the thought of sitting around the house all day with the wife. Perhaps this is all a big mistake. He's still vigorous. He can still contribute. The Dinosaur is reduced to begging. He even offers to stay on in a limited capacity as a Consultant. But it's no good—they want him gone. He's taking up too much real estate and can't work the fax machine. And so the Dinosaur retreats from his cubicle one last time, slips out without a festive sendoff, and is never heard from again.

MEMORABLE QUOTES

◆ "How many times do I need to ask you to keep it down?"

◆ "If [insert name of boss] sees you slacking off, he's just going to give us more work. Do you want more work? I sure don't."

◆ "Oh, great, another meeting with the brain trust. See you this afternoon."

PERFORMANCE REVIEW AND DEVELOPMENT REPORT

Employee: The Disinterested Secretary

> **Only the most significant and important points need to be recorded as a reference for the next review.**

The Disinterested Secretary's telephone headset allows her to gab with her girlfriends while simultaneously filing her nails or playing a few games of computer solitaire. She will look up long enough to engage her superiors with a blank stare but returns to her preferred endeavors the moment their backs are turned. Coworkers report that, though it is virtually impossible to hold a business-related conversation with her, the end result of the six hours she spent fiddling with her hair today is actually quite lovely.

The Disinterested Secretary is unfamiliar with the telephone system and the database used to store messages, though she is quite adept at flipping through fashion magazines and running out for quick visits to the snack machine. She has a tendency to zone out once talk turns from *Survivor* to any subject even slightly pertaining to business.

The Disinterested Secretary is simply too busy attending to the intricacies of her personal life to devote much brainpower or attention to her job. She planned her entire wedding on company time and recently eschewed sending a fax for her boss in favor of shopping online for anniversary presents. When not on the telephone or embroiled in a heated game of Free Cell, the Disinterested Secretary enjoys staring at the clock or painting her toenails.

She is a strong proponent of two-hour lunch breaks and recently petitioned the IT Guy to install three-way calling on her telephone. Fellow secretaries routinely pick up the slack for reasons they can't quite fathom or even identify.

Comments and Recommendations: Ill suited to office work of any kind; should switch to a career in homemaking at some point in the near future; how/why she was hired in the first place is anyone's guess.

PERFORMANCE REVIEW AND DEVELOPMENT REPORT

Employee: The Drama Queen

> **Only the most significant and important points need to be recorded as a reference for the next review.**

Either the Drama Queen is unfathomably incompetent or the mundane specifics of her lower administrative station are actually overwhelming enough to provide the impetus for a level of overwrought drama usually reserved for ancient Greek amphitheaters or public high school auditoriums. She greets any request for services ("Please file these"; "Could you get this person on the phone for me?"; "I'm going to need six copies of this") in the manner of a third-grader asked to walk the family dog (she initially pretends not to hear, then, when this tactic proves futile, resorts to performing the task as slooooooooooowly as possible, all the while rolling her eyes and dragging her feet).

The Drama Queen cannot sit still, and passes the day in fits of wildly projected tantrums. Even the simplest, most easily solved conundrums (her boss specifically requested that she order oatmeal raisin cookies for the afternoon meeting, but the bakery only has *chocolate chip*) are amplified by the Drama Queen into cause for panic. In fact, few events regularly encountered throughout the workday do not constitute some sort of crisis for her.

She employs various wild hand motions, narrowed eyes (meant to convey severe concentration), the rubbing of temples (ostensibly to soothe her stress-related headaches), and favorite phrases, such as "Oh, my God" or "This can't be happening" in a grand effort to both mask her inability to deal with ordinary events and convince coworkers of the heightened stress levels she must endure.

After several days of being confronted by the Drama Queen's bloodshot eyes and hypermanic disposition, coworkers undertake mass efforts to tune out not only her latest hyperbolic outburst but her very existence.

Comments and Recommendations: Future brain aneurism should finally rid the office of her presence.

PERFORMANCE REVIEW AND DEVELOPMENT REPORT

Employee: The Dreaded Lawyer

> **Only the most significant and important points need to be recorded as a reference for the next review.**

The Dreaded Lawyer occupies the office where ambition goes to die. A stickler for rules and procedures (however insignificant or obscure), he strikes fear into the hearts of his coworkers. Though he claims to be "just doing my job," it seems reasonable to question the character of a man whose job entails little more than crushing the hopes and dreams of those around him.

Rarely, if ever, invited to meetings, the Dreaded Lawyer is somehow cognizant of coworkers' plans to gather to discuss matters of an ambitious nature. He is devoid of all social hang-ups and will not hesitate to barge in on a closed-door meeting or make his concerns known via memo or e-mail. While certain lawyers are valued for their ability to, say, create due diligence in anticipation of a highly beneficial and creative merger, the Dreaded Lawyer accepts as his personal mission a strict adherence to the status quo (for example, he adamantly refuses to compensate volunteers, even though all evidence suggests that even the smallest stipend would increase productivity exponentially).

He employs an emotionless negative response in order to get his way and will stoop to citing the company's bylaws and operating procedures as necessary. Even when in the wrong, the Dreaded Lawyer's advanced mastery of minutiae is generally effective enough to thwart even the most brilliant, if unorthodox, proposals. Coworkers spend significant time avoiding him in the flesh and crafting intricate fail-safes designed to prevent the Dreaded Lawyer from catching wind of their plans. He is never, ever invited to happy hour and usually eats lunch at his desk alone.

The Dreaded Lawyer carries an umbrella every day and is rumored to store galoshes in the bottom drawer of his filing cabinet.

Comments and Recommendations: Has no desire to advance and in fact considers the prospect of promotion to constitute an unnecessarily risky proposition on par with airplane travel, Indian food, and creative problem solving; will remain in this position until he opts to retire.

THE FLOOZY

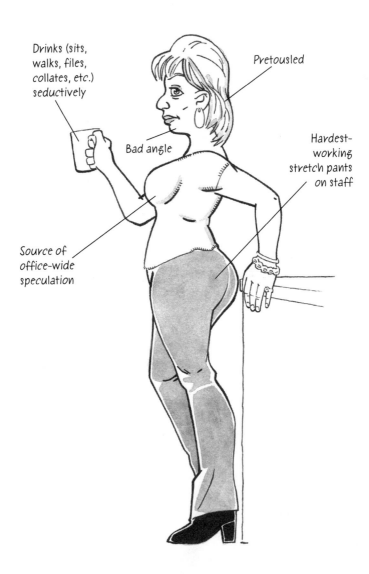

Drinks (sits, walks, files, collates, etc.) seductively

Pretousled

Bad angle

Hardest-working stretch pants on staff

Source of office-wide speculation

What would the office be like without its Floozy? Would productivity increase? Would the supply room door be locked less often? Would fewer memorandums re: Acceptable Corporate Dress need distributing? Who knows, and who cares? The Floozy is here to stay. As long as the boss is bored with his wife and paperwork needs attention, she will continue to sashay her way past your cube, distracting you with swiveling hips and the lingering scent of cheap perfume.

Like Christmas bonuses, Floozies come in many shapes and sizes. Sure, all dress in a wildly inappropriate manner and spend more time filing their nails than filing papers, but some are actually more risqué than others. Since all communication (both verbal and electronic) with the resident Floozy involves a decent amount of sexual innuendo, it is imperative to determine just how much of a bimbo your Floozy really is before attempting contact. After all, you'd hate to assume that the Floozy is up for a quickie in the conference room just because she happens to wear visible garters and thongs to work. Make one false move with the wrong Floozy and she'll cry sexual harassment faster than you can rebuckle your pants.

Wooing the Floozy can be a painstaking, delicate endeavor. It requires creativity, patience, and daring. Interested parties should master the art of the office-themed double entendre ("When you're finished filing, could you spend a little time under my desk?"), assume a position of authority (the Floozy is attracted to power), and establish a method of nonverbal cross-office communication utilizing only your eyebrows and lips (though the occasional chin rub may be mixed in to spice things up). But take it slowly. The Floozy can be more difficult to engage than the Red Baron.

Female coworkers tend to regard the Floozy with considerable disdain, due mainly to her ability to curry favor with management and sleep her way to the top (or, more accurately, to a position slightly higher than ability would suggest). For all the ladies out there, here's a simple way to defeat her: wait until the company barbecue, picnic, or holiday party (as the case may be); get the Floozy to ingest a preposterous amount of alcohol in a very short period of time; and get her on the dance floor. Allow her to make a complete mess and spectacle of herself in front of the head honcho and several important clients. She'll be gone by Monday.

Not only do certain Floozies hop into the supply closet at the drop of a hat, but they routinely relate the sordid details to fascinated (and often repulsed) coworkers. Sexual escapades with the right type of supervisor (that is, one "happily" married, quite high up the corporate ladder, and in possession of a no-questions-asked corporate expense card) can become a badge of honor. And, since monopolizing lunchtime chitchat can be quite a thrill, Floozies love to reveal the gory details of their transgressions to wide-eyed and scandalized coworkers. This is better than *Peyton Place*!

Since the office can be a lonely, mind-numbing, and horrible place to be, it's easy to find yourself (if you're male, lesbian, or just curious/bored) musing over physical contact with the Floozy. Even if she's sort of gross, it still beats data entry, right? So it can come as something of a depressing surprise that the recipient of her affections is often wildly unattractive and thoroughly uninteresting. The member of upper management fortunate enough to partake of the Floozy's charms usually boasts an aggressively receding hairline, doughy waistline, and a corporate wardrobe seemingly left over from an early season of

The Cosby Show. How these guys do it is anybody's guess. Oh, wait . . . they can fire people.

The most endearing quality of the Floozy is her preposterously ambitious future plans. Not that they are particularly dumb—but Floozies tend to profess career aspirations way, way, way out of reach (for most anyone). While clicking their gum and absentmindedly updating their calendars, many muse on becoming air traffic controllers or professional deep sea divers. Who knew administrative work was a gateway to such grand professions? Of course, in reality, most will just marry (usually some low-paid, brawny guy), settle down, and give birth to six or seven kids. At which time your office will become a much, much duller place to work.

MEMORABLE QUOTES

♦ "Germany has its own language?"

♦ "Anyone feel like mai tais at Applebee's for lunch?"

♦ "What, you don't have mistletoe in your cube?"

♦ "His wife thinks he was at a meeting."

PERFORMANCE REVIEW AND DEVELOPMENT REPORT

Employee: The Freelancer

> **Only the most significant and important points need to be recorded as a reference for the next review.**

To hear him tell it, the Freelancer is not actually employed by the company in any significant way, but merely shows up from 9:00 a.m. until 5:00 p.m., puts in a full day of work, and collects a biweekly paycheck. Excepting these trivial similarities to the average office drone, he bears little resemblance to anyone uninteresting enough to seek employment in or otherwise associate with corporate America. Furthermore, to the Freelancer, his practices of riding the train to work, dressing in business casual wear, and operating out of a cubicle somehow do not mean that he is exactly like a regular employee.

It is very important that all coworkers remain aware that he is a Freelancer, and that by this designation he intends to illustrate his status as a creative, progressive Bohemian type who just happens to spend forty to fifty hours per week shut up in an office. The Freelancer claims to be a writer, artist, or musician, though evidence of any such talents is sorely lacking. His dearth of substantive creative output, however, does not hinder him from pontificating on such topics as independent film, graphic design, and modern art. He enjoys reminding coworkers of the abysmal nature of their reading habits and considers his preference for flat-front (nonpleated) pants to constitute a lifestyle statement of overwhelming significance.

Unlike the Day Jobber, the Freelancer exhibits no actual artistic inclination other than a colorful ability to pass off fictional triumphs as real and a determination to deposit a hefty portion of his impressive corporate paycheck into the cash registers of trendy downtown hot spots. Though professing a studiously "edgy" preference for anarchy, he seems quite comfortable working for the same "Man" who keeps him down.

Comments and Recommendations: Need for health benefits should prompt him to come on board as a salaried employee before he turns thirty, though he will continue to lament Roger Ebert's "pedestrian" take on cinema.

PERFORMANCE REVIEW AND DEVELOPMENT REPORT

Employee: The Gossip

> **Only the most significant and important points need to be recorded as a reference for the next review.**

The Gossip has a tendency to get ahead of herself and, therefore, her speech is punctuated by a barely contained breathless quality. Her mind races from one delectable tidbit to the next, each of which holds her attention for precisely the time it takes to tell everyone in the office.

Though her sources are spotty (at best), her chronology out of whack, and her storytelling skills stuck on the third-grade level, the Gossip remains convinced that her ribald selections are nothing less than riveting. No one knows just where the Gossip gets her information, though she is thought to concoct the majority of it during her morning commute. The Gossip considers most banter of a professional variety disagreeable and prefers juicier and more scandalous subjects, such as the latest supply closet trysts, rumors of impending mass layoffs, and speculation as to the possibility that a fellow secretary recently had a boob job.

Though most coworkers entertain her in the hope that she will disappear once the story ends, the Gossip seems so convinced of their interest in the shocking nature of her information that she will sometimes consent to fill them in only under the condition that they lean in closely in order to appreciate the conspiratorial nature of her excited whispers. Once the transaction is complete, the Gossip excitedly moves on to the next cubicle, pausing only to flash the *shhhhhh* sign (forefinger upon lips) in parting.

Comments and Recommendations: Report that the CEO was caught under his desk with both his receptionist *and* his assistant (a narrative that somehow makes its way back to both the CEO's wife *and* his mistress) should severely limit her career options within the company.

PERFORMANCE REVIEW AND DEVELOPMENT REPORT

Employee: The *Groundhog Day* Guy

> **Only the most significant and important points need to be recorded as a reference for the next review.**

Named for the movie in which Bill Murray portrays a man reliving the same day over and over, the *Groundhog Day* Guy schedules weekly, one-on-one meetings at which the exact same information is reviewed as was the week prior. Coworkers rarely encounter the *Groundhog Day* Guy outside the context of such meetings, most likely because his entire workweek comprises nothing more than meeting with a vast, rotating list of employees. His official job description (or function) remains rather murky, though it is assumed that he is performing some specialized task at the behest of upper management.

Not only does the *Groundhog Day* Guy introduce the identical concepts and make the identical observations at each meeting, but he also goes so far as to produce a notepad filled with scribblings taken at the first such meeting, from which he pretends to "note" (really just hovering his pen millimeters above the already-written notations) the details of each weekly conversation. It usually takes coworkers a month or so to grow comfortable with the *Groundhog Day* Guy's pointlessness, after which they begin to anticipate their meetings with him as nice two-hour opportunities to slack off.

In addition to his fondness for rehashing stale concepts and mind-numbingly familiar professional observations for years on end, the *Groundhog Day* Guy is content to begin each meeting with a well-rehearsed round of small talk and conclude each session with a brief series of nondescript pleasantries designed to be applicable to all ("Have a wonderful weekend"; "Great meeting"; "I'm happy we had this opportunity to touch base"). Furthermore, the *Groundhog Day* Guy appears to wear the same outfit to work and devours a tuna sandwich (on white) at precisely 12:30 p.m. in the far left corner of the cafeteria each day.

Comments and Recommendations: Odds are, he will receive exactly the same comments on next year's review, just as he did last year and the year before.

THE GUNG-HO MBA

The Gung-Ho MBA absolutely loves to work. Really, he can't get enough. Sure, the Pompous General Partner may receive daily faxes while on vacation, but this joker works every Saturday (and most Sundays), gets home around eleven each night, and feels Christmas Day puts a kink in his professional plans. He is so into it that his casual wear is barely distinguishable from his work gear; even while he's "relaxing," shirts (even T-shirts!) will be tucked in and all pants will remain pleated. The Gung-Ho MBA dreads retirement not because he fears growing old but because he will have no idea what to do with himself.

Having spent upwards of twenty months attending a night or two of courses per week, the Gung-Ho MBA considers himself an expert on all aspects of the office's business. Sure, you've been with the company for twenty years, but come on, he got a B+ in Economics of Strategic Behavior. There is no subject outside the Gung-Ho MBA's sphere of expertise. He's even got a few ideas regarding the shoes you went with this morning.

Promptly after graduation, the Gung-Ho MBA develops a refined sense of taste usually reserved for heirs to the British throne. That old cubicle just isn't going to cut it anymore. He needs a big new office and a flat-screen computer monitor. A nice view wouldn't hurt, either. The thought of actually sharing an office or workspace is now as distasteful to the Gung-Ho MBA as the cut of a wide lapel. It's only a matter of time before he develops a taste for foxhunts and brandy. In keeping with his new upper-crust attitude, the Gung-Ho MBA will endeavor to keep the feudal system alive by treating his secretary like an unappreciated serf. In addition to actual secretarial skills, she will need to master the finer points of coffee brewing and treat fetching. Once in possession of his degree, the Gung-Ho MBA begins to regard his secretary more as a personal assistant than an administrative one. She will be placed in charge of his all-important personal datebook and ordered to "pick up a little something" for his girlfriend on their anniversary. Of course, this in no way means that her actual administrative tasks will ease up; such chores are simply beneath the contempt of the Gung-Ho MBA. His time is too valuable to bother with the nuts and bolts. The Gung-Ho MBA excels at breaking the backs of his assistants.

In addition to slave driving, the Gung-Ho MBA possesses a keen mastery of all Windows-based applications. While quite adept at Word, Excel, and Access, his real wizardry is reserved for PowerPoint. If you've ever seen Beethoven play piano, you can imagine how deft the Gung-Ho MBA is with the crafting of a PowerPoint presentation. PowerPoint is like oxygen to him; there is no concept he cannot display in a PP slide. The Gung-Ho MBA is something of an audiovisual savant, and his fluidity with a digital projector can be mesmerizing. Meetings hosted by the Gung-Ho MBA are similar in certain ways to a mid-1990s Pink Floyd concert.

In keeping with his love of employment, the Gung-Ho MBA is always "on." He is rarely seen without his game face and speaks only in combinations of trendy business buzzwords. The Gung-Ho MBA usually employs a fallback vocabulary of ten terms used to impress and hypnotize his boss and coworkers. Since few actually know what these terms mean, the Gung-Ho MBA is able to appear unbelievably intelligent and business-savvy. His bag of stock terminology usually involves at least several of the following: *aggregate, synergy, analysis, restructure, reengineer, boundarylessness, customer focus, cost driver, data warehouse, dovetail, macro, micro, business unit, integration, reorganize,* and *project lead.* And this doesn't even touch on his fondness for business-witty catchphrases, such as "Let's grab some low-hanging fruit," "Let's throw this against the wall and see if it sticks," or "Let's take this discussion offline." More often than not, the Gung-Ho MBA is in the thick of performing some type of analysis that nobody else can quite comprehend.

When not actually conducting business, the Gung-Ho MBA enjoys engaging in lighthearted banter with his coworkers. Though sports or girls are sometimes mentioned, he mostly prefers dropping the name of his Ivy League alma mater (God help you if you didn't attend at least a top 10 school) and ruminating on his future earning potential. When these fascinating topics run dry, the Gung-Ho MBA may move on to appraising the finer points of his signing bonus or detailing his plans to rule the entire business universe.

MEMORABLE QUOTES

◆ "In preparation for this presentation, we need to vet the outcome and really take a long look at the puts and takes. I would suggest holding a brainstorming session to really throw this against the wall and see if it sticks. After, I'll take the review upstairs and let management kick the tires before we submit to corporate. My reaction to the initial presentation is that we went around the block to get next door. Let's pare it down. As far as the other issue you want to discuss, I suggest a group of us get together and take it offline. Maybe we could even conduct an off-site meeting to be free of any distractions. Of course, let's first schedule a planning meeting to make sure we're all on the same page. I'll have Susie set it up."

◆ "Clearly, the discounted cash flows of this company exhibit a value that far exceeds that derived from precedent transactions."

◆ "I was at Columbia with the CFO's daughter."

PERFORMANCE REVIEW AND DEVELOPMENT REPORT

Employee: The Hall Monitor

> **Only the most significant and important points need to be recorded as a reference for the next review.**

We assume that the Hall Monitor does have a desk (or perhaps even an office), though the precise location of such a setting remains an absolute mystery. Coworkers happening upon the empty workstations sprinkled throughout the office occasionally wonder whether or not these hastily abandoned, wistfully depressing cubicles (resembling, as they do, the preserved interiors of Pompeii) may be the turf of the Hall Monitor, though such suppositions are rarely, if ever, proven true.

At first glance, the Hall Monitor appears capable of being in several places at once; then you realize that constant movement creates the illusion that he is conducting several simultaneous chitchats in practically every office corridor. It is virtually impossible to pass through the hallways without encountering the Monitor, to say nothing of the kitchen, men's room, copy room, water fountain, supply closet, lobby, or cafeteria.

The Hall Monitor spends the majority of his workday creating scenarios that enable him to get up and walk around the office without fear of question or reprimand. His favorite technique is to send a long and complicated project to the printer just so that he can repeatedly walk across the office to check on its progress.

Most troubling is his practice of cornering fellow workers in the hallway to conduct half-hour discussions of a personal nature. The exchange usually culminates with the Hall Monitor's signature flourish: a decision to escort the coworker back to his (the coworker's) cubicle while he finishes his story. If the duration of this walk proves insufficient to support the Hall Monitor's tale, he will stand at the edge of the cube until all pertinent information has been conveyed, successfully avoiding an additional six minutes of work.

Comments and Recommendations: Difficult to determine future prospects, as current function remains murky at best.

THE INCONTINENT CEO

Tucked away in a corner office of plush carpeting and stately wood, the Incontinent CEO lords over a kingdom of his own creation. It's been sixty-five years since he started (or took control of) the company, yet still he reigns. Though technology ("E-mail? What the hell are you talking about now?"), fashion ("Casual Friday? Humbug!"), and business custom ("Can you get together Wednesday for a three-hour martini lunch?") have all passed him by, the Incontinent CEO remains blissfully unaware of his own irrelevance. He is the master of his domain and is entrenched strongly enough to continue getting his way.

Once upon a time, well before you were even born, the Incontinent CEO was an ambitious, dashing, and brilliant young man. The countless photos of the boss in his prime lining the office hallways offer testament to his former glory (yes, that's him with Sophia Loren). And he was nothing if not refined: an expert on fine wine, food, and culture (this expertise, in fact, is his last remaining impressive feature). Oh, and don't forget his gorgeous wardrobe. He makes you feel ashamed of your own Dockers but, of course, doesn't pay you enough to buy better clothes. His physical demise and adamant refusal to retire are now the source of office-wide depression. It's bad enough to have to go to work every day, but who needs the constant reminder of their own mortality on top of everything else?

The Incontinent CEO's darkened Xanadu of an office resembles a hospital room in more ways than one (breathe through your mouth if possible), and his personal administrative assistant does more nursing than dictation. He requires constant attention and upkeep and can barely wipe his face after lunch; good luck getting him to focus long enough to entertain that raise you've requested.

Young employees marvel over the fact that he can't be forced out, but the Incontinent CEO is much savvier than that. A lifetime spent stacking the Board of Trustees with loyal cronies can do wonders for a man's professional longevity. And though rival factions have taken root and begun to rumble, they'll never get him in time. He's too wily for them, too smart, too . . . old. The man has one major lifestyle change left in him, and it doesn't involve ceding control of his empire to a bunch of sniveling business school grads. He is the last of the Old Guard and is committed to holding on, if only for the chance to assert his virility a little while longer. Sure, he's willing to lose the little battles from time to time. It's no longer acceptable behavior to pat his female employees on the butt as they pass by in the hall? Fine. The Incontinent CEO can live with that. This is a man who jumped out of airplanes over Europe; he's not about to be derailed by a little political correctness.

For all his physical shortcomings and antiquated notions, the Incontinent CEO is not a thoroughly reviled man. Unlike his more contemporary counterpart the Pompous General Partner, he does not inspire hatred or a desire to exact revenge. Most regard him as they would an elderly grandparent. However, though you love your grandfather, you wouldn't necessarily want him running your office, right? He's fine for holidays, the occasional dinner, a bimonthly phone call, but perhaps not so well equipped to weigh in on the ambitious merger you've dreamt up. Despising the Incontinent CEO would be a little like growing impatient with Benjamin Franklin over his lack of familiarity with the standard transmission in your Mini Cooper. He dates from a distinctly different time, and his only real sin is an inability to walk away.

MEMORABLE QUOTES

◆ "1922 was a very good year for me."

◆ "Has anyone seen my teeth?"

◆ "Get me Johnson on the transatlantic Dictagram posthaste."

PERFORMANCE REVIEW AND DEVELOPMENT REPORT

Employee: The Inhumane Human Resources Assistant

> **Only the most significant and important points need to be recorded as a reference for the next review.**

This self-important purveyor of vacation days and W-2 forms ironically lacks what should be her biggest asset: people skills. The Inhumane Human Resources Assistant excels at crafting an intricate maze of bureaucracy, the main effect of which is to render her own workday free of any actual work.

For example, certain urban offices provide employees with vouchers for the cost of public transportation. Said vouchers need to be submitted on a monthly basis to HR in order for compensation to be distributed. However, the generosity of this policy is often undermined by the Inhumane Human Resources Assistant's decision to accept vouchers only according to a slim and ever-changing schedule, the particulars of which are rarely posted in plain sight. Employees who miss the forty-five-minute window of opportunity are out of luck until next month.

The IHRA takes gaudily lengthy lunch breaks, uses personal days (of which she appears to have an unlimited supply) for reasons most employees would never dream (such as having her nails done), and refuses to act on personnel complaints of even the most egregious nature (such as a certain much more attractive female coworker's report of sexual harassment). The Inhumane Human Resources Assistant greets coworkers who approach her for assistance with some condescending or catty remark ("Well, I've seen those short skirts you wear . . ."), followed soon after by the collected giggling of the sewing-circle-like Human Resources department at large.

Defeated, coworkers head back to their desks with their heads hanging low and still having no real idea of how to invoke their rights or enroll in the company's 401(K) plan.

Comments and Recommendations: Command of useless bureaucratic skills indicates a future career in state government, perhaps at the DMV.

PERFORMANCE REVIEW AND DEVELOPMENT REPORT

Employee: The Know-It-All

> **Only the most significant and important points need to be recorded as a reference for the next review.**

The Know-It-All is the loudest human being in the office. It would be reasonable to assume that he achieves such volume by employing some amplification device, such as a megaphone or karaoke machine, but in fact that is his natural pitch. Coworkers whose workstations line the office's outer wall have reported being able to hear the Know-It-All from as far away as his regular parking space in the lot's second tier. He rarely, if ever, finds it necessary to telephone a colleague or drop in for a face-to-face encounter when a shout across the office will do just fine.

The Know-It-All professes to be an expert on all official business, as well as on the personal lives of his coworkers. His guttural, booming voice is as imposing an instrument whether used to second-guess the Consultants' advice, lambaste his secretary for her inability to instantly grasp his latest brainstorm, or ridicule a certain hapless coworker for his admittedly shortsighted decision to remarry his ex-wife.

There is no topic of conversation with which the Know-It-All seems unfamiliar. In the span of a single lunch break, he has been known to pontificate on the perils of Martian exploration, the effects of triangular trade routes on the socioeconomic development of the eastern seaboard, your spouse's reaction to the anniversary gift you've just purchased (not good), the specific statistical performance of Sandy Koufax had he pitched today, and the boss's rumored attempt to merge the company with a larger entity.

The Know-It-All will not pause to allow coworkers to register their reactions, but instead plows from one subject to the next until he needs to visit the men's room. It is estimated that at least 85 percent of the Know-It-All's musings are 100 percent misinformed.

Comments and Recommendations: Ask him.

THE LAME DUCK

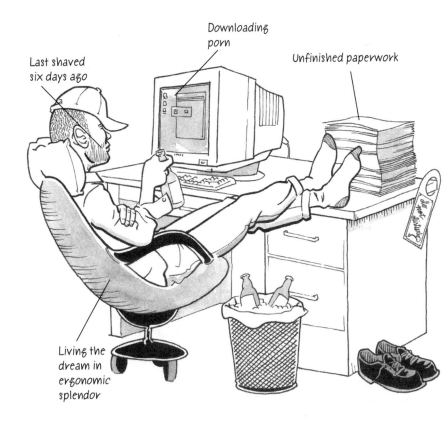

Having just given his two weeks' notice, the Lame Duck has a new and glorious lease on life. In our wildest dreams we can't begin to imagine possessing his cavalier attitude. Here is a man whose actions bear no consequence. A man brazen enough to wear shorts to work (and not on Hawaiian Day). A man with a life-altering mantra at his disposal: "What are they gonna do, fire me?" Not even the Temp does less work than the Lame Duck, and we all know how impressively lazy the Temp can be.

Everyone on staff is eligible for Lame Duck–hood; the lone requirement being a willingness to resign. Whether upper management or lowly administrative drone, the joys and benefits of becoming a Lame Duck are available to all. The position requires no training, the hours are flexible, and actual job-related tasks are kept to a strict minimum. In fact, the only drawback to becoming a Lame Duck is the brevity of the experience. It's amazing how quickly two workweeks zip by when you're not actually doing any work. Equally surprising is how much fun the office can be when you're just there to chitchat, surf the Web, and stock up on items from the supply closet.

Once he has made the leap and become a Lame Duck, even the once despised boss seems like an old friend he's almost sorry to soon lose contact with. And the office, well, the office might as well be the boss's lovely and well-appointed winter retreat. Should the Lame Duck need to make a few long distance calls of a personal nature? No problem. The Lame Duck's feeling sleepy? Well, he can go right ahead and take a nap at his desk. He's earned it. What's that? He'd like a drink? Well, he can help himself. There's beer in the fridge. Sure, drink it in the conference room—that's no problem. What are they gonna do, fire him?

Some Lame Ducks get so comfortable that to the untrained eye they may appear to have just wandered in off the slopes, bundled up in a comfy sweater and blowing the steam off a mug of cocoa. A favorite Lame Duck activity is extending three-hour lunch invitations to colleagues, then scoffing at their inability to attend. In addition to their aforementioned favorite phrase, Lame Ducks are fond of the old standby "What, is the earth gonna stop spinning if you don't [blank]?" Depending on industry, this blank can be filled in with "file those expense reports," "analyze that merger," "prepare for the quarterly stockholders meeting," or "work until five." The question is always accompanied by bemused chuckling and is followed by the Lame Duck wandering away, shaking his head in disbelief. In some extreme cases, he may top the conversation off by observing, "I don't know how you do it."

Of course, there are a few things the Lame Duck does actually need to take care of before he leaves. There's that desk to clean out, and he supposes he should meander down to HR at some point for that exit interview everyone's talking about. Also, it's gonna take some time to say goodbye to everybody. And, worst of all, the Lame Duck needs to spend twenty minutes or so deleting personal files from his computer. But still, most of these chores can be completed in a single day. Most Lame Ducks prefer saving it all for their second-to-last day, usually a Thursday. This gives them eight solid days of not working and saves their very last Friday for a display of slacking off the likes of which you haven't seen since Rip Van Winkle settled in for a little snooze.

The Lame Duck begins his last day by strolling in around noon, dressed in T-shirt, sweat pants, sneakers, and carrying a half-eaten bag of Cooler Ranch Doritos. He then proceeds to munch his way toward his desk, stopping briefly to poke his head into the boss's office to inquire as to the status of his superior's golf handicap. The Lame Duck will then spend a half hour or so blatantly flirting with the secretaries before unwinding with a few cocktails in his cubicle. After a short respite at the front desk to turn in his ID card and ogle women with the Security Guards, the Lame Duck sends an office-wide, semi-insulting goodbye e-mail message before taking off around three-thirty, never to be seen or heard from again.

Of course, management stands firmly and officially opposed to both personal expression and freedom of thought. The powers that be want nothing more than to rain on the Lame Duck's parade, to crush him with administrative duty. Sometimes it's too late to act and the Lame Duck wins. But certain supervisors can be quite crafty and will stop at nothing to crush the souls of all who work for them. Such supervisors possess one diabolical weapon they will not hesitate to deploy: the Protégée. A new hire acquired to replace the departing employee, the Protégée will bring the briefly triumphant Lame Duck crashing down to earth. After all, the Protégée needs training, and who better to perform the task than the person most familiar with the position? Oh, it's underhanded, all right. It's sneaky and awful and unjust. But what can a Lame Duck do? Well, mope, for one thing. And roll his eyes, for another. But then what? Desperate times call for desperate measures, and the Lame Duck has one option left to him: an absentminded, disinterested two weeks of "training" sure to guarantee that the Protégée is worse at her job than had she received no training at all.

And so the Lame Duck departs, laughing all the way to his next dreadful occupation.

MEMORABLE QUOTES

◆ The Protégée: "So, how should I prepare for the project meeting?"

The Lame Duck: "Eh, just wing it."

◆ "You guys feel like knocking off early? . . . [chuckles] . . . sorry, I forgot you still work here."

◆ "I'd love to help you out, but I'm due for a nap in Conference Room C."

THE LETHARGIC EXCUSE FOR A FILLED POSITION

Granted, everyone in their right mind hates to work, but the Lethargic Excuse for a Filled Position not only refuses to toil but actually sneers at her supervisor for having the audacity to suggest such a thing. Once a productive member of the workforce, the Lethargic Excuse for a Filled Position lost the will to work after a decade or so spent performing various mindless tasks for supervisors who took the effort for granted. Since it has become virtually impossible to fire someone unless they either mug a nun or embezzle from the retirement fund, management has decided that it's easier to assign work to someone else than constantly reprimand the Lethargic Excuse, whose responsibilities eventually dwindle to bathing before work and not breaking any office equipment.

You, on the other hand, have done a really bang-up job since being hired straight out of college. The boss is impressed with your energy and ability to flirt with important clients. He rewards you with a nice little promotion. For the first time, you'll have someone working directly under you. Enter the Lethargic Excuse for a Filled Position. Of course, you've never met her before. She was off lurking in some faraway department or hiding in her cubicle. You try to get things off on the right foot and summon her to your new office. The Lethargic Excuse for a Filled Position finally shows up sulking in your doorway after you leave three or four messages. "Yeah?" Interesting, you think: no pleasant "Hello, what can I do for you?" Perhaps she's just shy.

The relationship between the Lethargic Excuse and her immediate supervisor quickly devolves into an awkward routine of "she said / she said." First of all, the Lethargic Excuse never returns phone calls. She will respond to a fifth message, but only via e-mail. Of course, this response will contain roughly half of the requested info, forcing you to go back and ask for everything again a few more times. To finally acquire the desired information, the Lethargic Excuse will resort to methods that take twice as long and that simultaneously make the company look bad. For example, if you request a customer's account number, the Lethargic Excuse will proceed to contact the customer to ask for it instead of just looking it up through normal intraoffice methods. What's more, the Lethargic Excuse will not hesitate to concoct fictional information to save herself the trouble of finding real answers.

The above scenario occurs only in the event that you actually manage to assign or request work from the Lethargic Excuse, who knows no equal when it comes to staving off professional tasks before they can be requested. Her ability to shirk responsibility relies on a two-pronged counterattack: the Lethargic Excuse employs (no pun intended) confrontational methods to intimidate her superior while at the same time constructing an elaborate ruse to appear already busy. The former is achieved through the collection of wearied physical gestures she has at her disposal: rolled eyes, heavy exhalations, downturned mouth, plodding footsteps, shaking head, and tsk-tsk sounds add up to keep even the most persistent supervisors at bay. The latter depends on a creative streak possibly picked up designing sets for high school theater. The Lethargic Excuse creates the appearance of an overworked employee by cluttering her desk with all manner of busyness: papers (possibly pulled from the recycling bin), files, memos, Post-it notes, and office supplies. By the time she's finished, her cubicle looks like a Florida trailer park during hurricane season. The Lethargic Excuse has a sixth sense that allows her to anticipate the arrival of her boss, at which point she digs into the overflowing piles and assumes a crazed, stressed-out expression.

Sometimes, however, work just really needs to be done and you manage to cut through the Lethargic Excuse's trickery and assign a new project. This rarely goes over well. The Lethargic Excuse will lash out in anger like a cornered animal and look at you as if you just vomited slugs all over the floor. She will gesture to the stack of paper on her desk and act incredulous that anyone could possibly handle more. She will eventually calm down, throw the new work on top of a pile, and spend the rest of the day making meaningless trips to the copy machine. The Lethargic Excuse resents being assigned even the most minor tasks, such as collecting money for the office Christmas party.

MEMORABLE QUOTES

◆ [Blank stare.] "Oh, um . . . I e-mailed you on that a long time ago. You don't have it?!?"

◆ [Sigh.] "Well, I sent it . . . let me look through my sent mail."

◆ "Oh. I guess I never responded. Well . . . I'll look into that now."

PERFORMANCE REVIEW AND DEVELOPMENT REPORT

Employee: The Loud Mom

> **Only the most significant and important points need to be recorded as a reference for the next review.**

Billy forgot to pick up his goddamn sister from soccer practice. Susan can't stay out of trouble at school. The babysitter is apparently too stupid to warm the baby's milk before giving it to him. Or so was reported by the Loud Mom's coworkers, most of whom spent the better part of the afternoon distracted by her impossibly loud, unceasingly awful domestic goings-on.

Though it's unclear whether or not she will actually carry through on promises to "kick ass" and teach her children "a lesson" just as soon as she gets home, her venomous diatribes were sufficiently convincing when heard through the thin, imitation plastic walls of her cubicle that several fellow Administrative Assistants debated reporting the events to Children's Protective Services before ultimately deciding not to get involved.

The Loud Mom is able to conduct her professional duties (maintaining her boss's calendar, faxing, filing, data entry) while simultaneously berating her deadbeat teenage son over the telephone. During lunch and coffee breaks, she plods heavily about the cafeteria (or break room), occasionally rolling her eyes, shrugging her shoulders, or, apropos of very little, lamenting her decision to get knocked up in high school.

Superiors regret their inability to provide some sort of counseling or to fire her but admit that they're more than a little intimidated by her temper. It remains unlikely that the Loud Mom's situation will improve at any point in the foreseeable future, save for some unfortunate catastrophe involving the entire brood and a steep mountain pass.

Comments and Recommendations: Should hold current position for the remainder of her career, assuming she continues to elude child abuse charges.

THE MAILROOM MILITIA

Is there anything worse than going to the post office? Well, cleaning the toilet kind of sucks. And unpacking a suitcase is no day in bed with Paris Hilton. What about waking up for work? That certainly rivals a trip to the post office. But what if there was a way to combine the horror of your ringing alarm clock with the misery of waiting in line for half an hour to mail a package? Welcome to the wonderful world of dealing with the Mailroom Militia.

A lazier group of people you will not find at the office, with the possible exception of certain Temps. Members of the Mailroom Militia schedule short, fleeting moments of actual work around the smoking and chatting breaks that constitute the majority of their day. Not that this should be a reason to dislike them. After all, who wouldn't rather smoke cigarettes than work? It's a no-brainer, which perfectly describes members of the Militia, as well. Sure, to wind up as an office drone you must have done a little slacking off somewhere along the way yourself, but at least the party school you attended technically qualifies as higher education. The Mailroom Militia is not known for its intellectual prowess.

What they are known for is regularly losing the mail you ask them to send and forgetting to deliver the mail you receive. Persuading a member of the Militia to perform a professional duty can prove more challenging than persuading the Pompous General Partner to adopt a four-day workweek. And, if you do manage to get them to do something like, say, close up a box with some packing tape, understand that the Militia expects to be compensated a little extra for such chores, as if it's not already a part of their job. The Mailroom Militia is worse than hotel porters when it comes to expecting a little gratuity for their efforts. Not that you'll actually need to tip them in cash (if you do, dip into the petty cash), but you may need to throw a little emotional largesse their way. The Mailroom Militia will hold you in contempt if you don't act as if they just saved your newborn from a runaway truck every time they stamp an envelope.

Members of the Mailroom Militia are most frequently spotted (when outside the actual mailroom) wheeling their metallic mail carts around the office. More often than not, you will encounter one on the elevator, where he will insist on squeezing in no matter how crowded the space already is. After causing everyone onboard to scrunch into one far corner of the car, he will then proceed to ride only as far as the next floor. They are also fond of clipping some outrageously large cell phone or walkie-talkie to their belts, and, if the latter, it will squawk incessantly, like a cop's CB radio. Apparently the inner workings of the mailroom are quite complex and require constant verbal communication.

The mailroom proper consists of little more than a very large, open room distinguished by vast worktables, packing materials, and boom boxes (usually set to top volume). Gaining access to the mailroom can prove more difficult than bypassing Studio 54's velvet rope circa 1978. Instead, you will be required to conduct all business through a tiny window designed specifically for such purposes. Of course, the Militia member at this window will rarely deign to look up from her magazine to acknowledge your presence.

Even though the Militia couldn't care less about the office and strives to do the absolute minimum at all times, they are real sticklers for rules and regulations when such procedures can be used to annoy the hell out of you. For example, if you come to the window looking for a package you're expecting, it can be sitting right there in plain sight and they won't give it to you due to some obscure office bylaw compelling them to deliver all mail directly to employees' desks. Infuriating.

Some offices don't have an actual mailroom, and at these locales the duties of the Militia are performed by a moonlighting Receptionist. Usually, this setup requires the existence of a UPS or FedEx workstation available to all employees. You just need to fill out the "To:" section of the shipping label; the Receptionist will take care of the rest (just leave it on her desk). She is also capable of tracking packages you neurotically believe are taking too long to arrive. In these situations, the UPS/FedEx delivery guy becomes a regular part of the office. He pops in at least once a day, exchanges a few pleasantries with the Receptionist, and is privy to all office gossip. You can set your watch to his comings and goings.

The following is very rare, but worth mentioning: the Mailroom Militia can be such a pain to deal with that certain offices opt to replace it entirely with the Robot Mailman. Resembling a discarded droid from *Star Wars,* the Robot Mailman is basically a library magazine rack on wheels. Traveling through the office at stupendously slow speed (though not quite as slow as actual human Militia members), the Robot Mailman "delivers" and "picks up" mail according to a predetermined route. Actually, it is your responsibility to place or retrieve mail from the Robot's shelves without being run over, though the system can be surprisingly reliable. Of course, the Robot is incapable of action more sophisticated than simple delivery and retrieval, so the office must still employ some yahoo to sit in a back room and sort the mail. Still, the Robot can be a grim reminder that someday soon you will be completely phased out by the machines.

MEMORABLE QUOTES

◆ "Hey, buddy, this ain't the friggin' post office."

◆ "We can't handle packages over two pounds."

◆ "I got my GED for this?"

THE MAN WHO WOULD BE KING

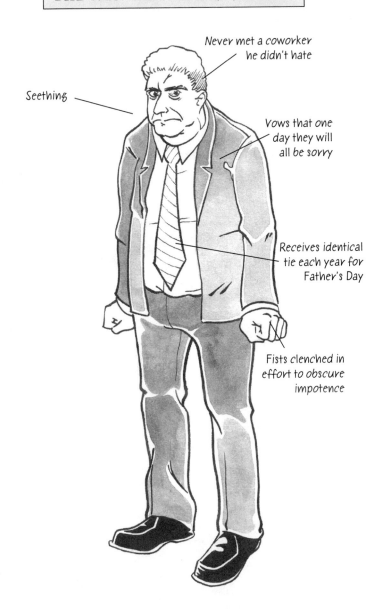

Never met a coworker
he didn't hate

Seething

Vows that one
day they will
all be sorry

Receives identical
tie each year for
Father's Day

Fists clenched in
effort to obscure
impotence

He has bided his time for all these years, sat patiently awaiting the boss's death or incapacitation. He asks himself, "How long can a man possibly hang on? And why won't he just retire? Is that too much to ask?" The Man Who Would Be King sits in his cluttered office, staring at the clock and brooding. He plays by the rules, wears a tie and starched shirt every day, shuffles right by you in the hallway without saying hello. The Man Who Would Be King is ready to snap.

The Man Who Would Be King is not employed by a large corporation but toils in a smallish office of twenty or so tortured souls. He is the president's right-hand man and the enforcer of corporate rules and regulations. He is humorless when it comes to the inner workings of the office (and most other topics as well). Technically, he may be an accountant or vice president, but the Man Who Would Be King's unofficial job description entails little more than carrying out the aging boss's latest whims, his blood pressure mounting.

It is rumored that the Man Who Would Be King has a wife and several children, though evidence of their existence is anecdotal at best. He is not one to decorate his desk with photos or to make telephone calls of a personal nature while at work. It is entirely possible that the MWWBK has not even shared his office number with his family. He has no time for trivial concerns; waggishly nodding his head "yes," scowling, and conducting a deathwatch require his undivided attention.

Unlike the rest of the office, the MWWBK is not interested in chitchat. If you wish him good morning he will merely grunt, put his head down, and ignore you. His best friend is a calculator, and he's not someone to whom you should bother extending a happy hour invitation. Not that he is one to hang around after work, anyway. Deep down, he knows he'll never be promoted, and so as soon as the clock strikes five, and not one second later, the Man Who Would Be King is out the door, his overcoat flapping behind him like a cape. This is a man who's given Judaism some serious thought merely for the potential increase in holiday time. He enjoys a special rapport with the elevator; it is always there when he needs it, awaiting him with open arms and rescuing him from the misery of unnecessary small talk with his coworkers. He wants to run the show, but, failing that, he can barely stand to spend another second in the office.

For all his efforts, the Man Who Would Be King will never be granted keys to the kingdom; when a changing of the guard finally does occur (as it inevitably must), he will remain the trusted Number Two. A new and energetic young boss will be recruited, and the Man Who Would Be King will be asked to welcome and assist him however possible, to ensure that the transition goes smoothly. Privately, he will recoil. Behind the increasingly closed door to his office, the Man Who Would Be King ties his tie even tighter, refuses all phone calls, and paces like a man with big ideas (of which he has none). He is middle aged and going nowhere. To make himself feel better, the Man Who Would Be King orders a young Administrative Assistant to assemble a computer desk, just because he can.

Like Pharaoh in Egypt, the Man Who Would Be King cares little for the just treatment of his fellow humans. He is particularly harsh on Interns and other young volunteers "employed" by the company. He works them to the bone, unimpressed by the spectacle or quality of their labor. Though their immediate supervisors approach him pleading for charity, the Man Who

Would Be King pompously brushes them away. If he is to be miserable, everybody will be miserable.

And so the Man Who Would Be King, unable to achieve much in his own life, resorts to crushing the spirits of those around him. He is particularly fond of refusing to provide health insurance and takes great pleasure in darkening even the lightest of moments. As the man in charge of the office's nuts and bolts, it is he you'll have to visit upon announcing your resignation. So you stop by the Man Who Would Be King's office, as much to say goodbye as to perform any official transaction. You'd like to shake hands, let bygones be bygones, walk out on a high note. The Man Who Would Be King will have none of it. He is incapable of being the bigger man, of taking the higher ground. Hearing of your bright future plans, he will respond, "You realize you won't be welcomed back, right?" Just ignore him. Everyone else does.

MEMORABLE QUOTES

♦ "I don't want to see you wearing sneakers tomorrow."

♦ "Columbus Day is not a paid holiday."

♦ "We're not going to increase your pay. You're lucky to have a job."

THE MICROMANAGER

Spent two hours obsessing over this cuff

Poised to harass

Pencils parallel to edge of desk

Stapler labeled "Property of"

The coworker whose breath you're most likely to smell over your shoulder, the Micromanager is anal retentive to the point of impotency and is the sworn enemy of all who come in contact with him. The Micromanager simply cannot delegate and must go into excruciating detail when describing even the most simplistic of concepts. Ignored and neglected during his youth, the Micromanager now *needs* to make sure he's got your undivided attention. Is this clear? Do you understand? Are you sure? Do you need him to show you? Here, let him have a crack at that so he can demonstrate exactly what he means. No, not like that. Like this. Let him explain it to you like you're a child. In case it's still not getting through, the Micromanager will be only too happy to repeat everything a few million more times.

The Micromanager gets nervous when forced outside the friendly confines of his office, a comforting, well-organized space where the highlighters are placed just so, perfectly parallel to the edge of his desk. When in doubt, he likes to assure himself that his vast network of file folders is indeed alphabetized, with each folder clearly labeled in crisp black ink. If, heaven forbid, the Micromanager happens to crease the tab of a folder while rifling through them, well, then, a new package will need to be opened and all the folders replaced. It's as simple as that.

The Micromanager possesses a gravitational pull greater than the sun's. Despite your best efforts, there is no way to avoid him. He lives in constant fear that whatever responsibilities he's been entrusted with will soon be snatched away, and so needs to remain actively involved with every tiny piece of the puzzle to ensure that things go smoothly. Of course, his preferred method of quality control (i.e., nitpicking) inevitably slows down the completion of each project without actually improving the chances of its success. Every word you write is an opportunity for the Micromanager to get involved. Send him a document, then steel yourself for the series of preposterously unnecessary comments (written in red) soon to land on your desk: "Why don't we change 'because' to 'due to'?" or "regarding" to "concerning" or "cat" to "feline"? There, isn't that better? Even work supposedly delegated your way will require that the Micromanager sign off on it before it moves forward. "Sign off" is, in fact, his favorite phrase. Of course, what this really means is that your report will sit on his desk for a month until it becomes outdated, at which point the Micromanager will request that you "update this before it can be signed off on," ensuring the cycle's continuation. After a while, it will seem as if you can't take a dump without the Micromanager signing off on it.

Why doesn't he just do the work himself in the first place? That's like asking why the cow jumped over the moon or how Boston can suck so badly. Nobody knows. Not that underlings don't ponder this mystery on a regular basis. Some, finally exasperated to the point of snapping, actually confront the Micromanager, who can only stagger about in wide-eyed confusion, like a character who bumps into his future self in a bad time-travel movie. There's no logical explanation for his behavior; he can't help it. Just like he can't help but painstakingly second-guess every move a cabdriver makes from the backseat or give the IT Guy more than six seconds to fix all his computer problems. He will eventually double back and reinstruct you on the particulars of whatever it is he's already asked for, as if the problem entails a lack of comprehension on your part. Bring a large mug of coffee; you'll need it to remain awake through the Micromanager's latest soliloquy (delivered in a monotone reminiscent of the HAL computer in *2001*).

Working directly under the Micromanager can result in loss of confidence, strong resentment of the company, and an impressive ability to perform keenly observed comedy routines detailing his personal and physical blemishes (which just kill with the happy hour crowd). In a more professional sense, the Micromanager's assistants slowly come to realize that he is motivated less by identifying (and solving) real problems than by pissing on projects to mark his territory. They eventually lose their joie de vivre and come to hate everything about the Micromanager: his tiny neat handwriting (which allows him to cram as much instruction as possible onto one Post-it note), his spreadsheets full of tedious and hyperdetailed analysis no one will ever need, his furiously pressed slacks. He can make even the most ambitious and idealistic employee grow to hate everything about the office.

MEMORABLE QUOTES

◆ "Did you run that e-mail through spell-check before you sent it?"

◆ "I'd recommend two sugars in that coffee."

◆ "I don't know why you don't align the icons on your desktop to the left. Here, let me see that mouse . . . watch this: I just click and drag them over. See? They're much easier to deal with this way."

THE NOCTURNAL CLEANING CREW

Back slightly bent from labor

Last-ditch effort to retain some cultural dignity

Company-issue smock

Enough inside information to destroy company

Garbage can is more spacious than apartment in Old Country

The Nocturnal Cleaning Crew toils behind the scenes like an industrious band of elves. They are often invisible, mysterious—perhaps imaginary. Yet somebody must be emptying your garbage can, right? And that urinal didn't clean itself. Like all good help, the Nocturnal Cleaning Crew lets its actions speak for themselves. They take pride in a job well done, and don't need to be complimented by the daytime staff. Of course, they don't speak English and wouldn't understand the compliment anyway, but still.

Certain members of the NCC are occasionally spotted in daylight. You may, for example, have encountered them and their cleaning carts in the elevator. Here's a fun way to pass the awkward moment: avert your gaze and pretend to be suddenly fascinated by your own shoes or mesmerized by the elevator buttons' corresponding Braille inscriptions. Blind people ride elevators? Who knew? This is something you can ponder while awaiting the ride's end.

If there's one thing worse than using an office bathroom (that is, unless you're fortunate enough to possess keys to the fabled executive washroom), it's cleaning one. This is the one task that the NCC prefers to perform during regular business hours. The motivation behind this discrepancy remains unclear, though perhaps what's going on here is a little simple revenge. As retaliation for having to wipe down the thrones of corporate drones or lift soggy sports sections up off the tile floor, the NCC has developed a knack for showing up to clean the bathroom at the precise moment you need to use it really, really badly. And who can relax and take care of business with all that commotion going on in there? It's enough to make you seriously rethink those tacos you've spent all morning craving. If you're lucky, bathrooms might be available on another floor or in a different department. If not, you're screwed. You will relieve yourself when and where the NCC deems such action possible.

These days Eastern European countries produce office cleaners the way they once produced suspiciously muscular female athletes. Regardless of locale, your office is no doubt kept tidy by a small team of recent defectors, which can actually be quite a comfort. By convincing yourself that this crappy job must represent some improvement over the dismal conditions of their homelands, it's possible to rationalize sticking that piece of gum to the outside of your garbage can. Of course, suppositions like these are usually made by office workers whose knowledge of world culture is limited to a honeymoon jaunt to EPCOT.

When you stop and think about it, working the night shift has some obvious advantages. Namely, no boss. But also free access to unlimited office supplies and a nicely stocked fridge. And you know what? Those couches out in the lobby, the ones nobody ever sits on? They're comfy! Lying there with a can of Coke, hanging out with your buddies, reminiscing about the old country; this is pretty damn good. Better than temping, anyway. Clean out a few cubicles, do a little sweeping, then sit back and relax. The Receptionist is usually required to clean the kitchen (sucker), so the NCC doesn't even need to bother with that. This ain't so bad.

The NCC can, however, take things a bit far. Male members are especially notorious for surfing pornographic Web sites on your computer while you're home tucking in the kids. Take a look at your browser history sometime. Or maybe don't. People get fired for this sort of thing. In addition to porn, the

NCC is quite fond of strange, practically indecipherable Web sites thought to detail the bizarre customs, culture, and history of smallish, politically unstable foreign lands.

One more thing about the NCC: don't mess with them. They have powerful friends in powerful places (such as the building's management company), friends who will not hesitate to dash off an incriminating memo to your supervisor if, say, you continue to use your cube as a personal storage locker. The NCC is not to be trifled with. These are people who have stood in line for bread. They are not impressed by the lack of closet space in your apartment.

MEMORABLE QUOTES

◆ "бы лучше еще десять лет в Гулаге отсидел, чем на работу завтра выходить."

◆ "Mere paas ek mercedes aur do ghar darya ke paas huwa karte the."

◆ "Czy ci ludzie nic nie robą tylko srają cały dzień?"

PERFORMANCE REVIEW AND DEVELOPMENT REPORT

Employee: The Nodder

> **Only the most significant and important points need to be recorded as a reference for the next review.**

The first to arrive at the conference table for meetings large and small, the Nodder takes great pains to situate himself in a high-profile seat directly beside the speaker. He requires twenty minutes or so of prep time to erect an intricate, highly important-looking structure of nonsensical objects (stacks of paper, scribbled-on legal pads, several freshly sharpened pencils, silver Cross pen, article clippings, multicolored printouts, file folders, etc.) on the table in front of him.

Throughout the meeting's entirety, the Nodder lives up to his name by engaging in a ritual of affirmative head movement. The Nodder's nods, though they also signal his strong endorsement of the speaker's agenda, serve primarily to illustrate his own impressive understanding of the business at hand. His motions suggest a familiarity not only with standard company procedure, but also with each highly specialized statement made by visiting Consultants and software analysts.

Whether or not he truly possesses some innate grasp of the material is a conclusion difficult to ascertain based solely on his actual work output, but his habit of periodically complimenting his nods with chin rubbings and eyebrow raisings certainly seems to suggest that the Nodder truly is some sort of corporate savant. He also employs these tactics to similar effect while listening to descriptions of his wife's day over dinner.

Comments and Recommendations: Perfect upper-management material.

Ah, the Office Girls: friends and confidantes to lowly Temps and uppity bosses alike. A gaggle of youngish females stuck forever in cubicles adjacent to their superiors' corner offices (sometimes referred to, collectively, as the Secretarial Pool), Office Girls are the company's most dedicated and least compensated employees. You've no doubt absentmindedly smiled at photos of their goateed husbands or barked lunch orders in their general direction. Nine to five, they are your wife, your babysitter, your secretary, your cheerleader, your memory, your mother, and your conscience.

Office Girls yearn for domestic bliss. There are exceptions, but most vacation at Disney World and coo aggressively over any infant brought to work. In fact, Temps routinely find employment filling in for Office Girls on maternity leave. Unfortunately, many Office Girls have yet to actually bear children and must settle for obsessing over the offspring of older sisters or sisters-in-law. Their overwhelmingly strong maternal instincts can come in quite handy on the job, as many bosses, not unlike toddlers, require constant maintenance.

If you've ever worked closely with the Office Girls, you know that they possess an incredible knack for mastering any task even remotely related to their profession. These Girls keep the office humming; they are adept at answering phones, scheduling appointments, maintaining databases, ordering supplies, booking conference rooms, playing computerized Free Cell, performing light copy-machine maintenance (including toner replacement), filing, ordering cars, making lunch reservations, soothing nerves, stroking egos, feigning interest in the lives of their boss's children, deciphering accents, keeping Rolodexes, eating lunch at their desks, sending packages, watering the office plants, and dealing with the building's maintenance and security staffs. Without them, business would screech to a halt in a matter of days. Of course, it is their very indispensability as underlings that prevents most from ever being promoted.

Office Girls are not necessarily identical to secretaries, despite the term "executive assistant" being regarded as mere overblown hogwash on par with, say, "waste technician." Actually, Office Girls need not be executive assistants (or secretaries) at all. Some hold actual lower-level management positions and, in fact, Office Girls are defined more by their group dynamic than by their job status. They function as a social club within the greater office hierarchy and seem the best of girlfriends, though the relationship rarely extends beyond the office (excepting such occasions as weddings, holiday parties, and happy hours).

Imagine the perkiest young woman in your office, then multiply her by four. Or, if it helps, think of whoever's organizing your high school reunion. This is what it's like to be among the Office Girls. They are nothing if not chipper, and they possess the stamina of people who actually go to bed at a decent hour and begin the day with a square breakfast. In their sweater sets, slacks, and makeup (reapplied liberally in the ladies' room during lunch break), Office Girls carry the emotional burden for the rest of the staff. Despite a complete lack of personal stake in the company's business, they express sincere excitement whenever a deal is struck, an investment pans out, or a positive quarter is reported. Likewise, they take negative corporate news personally, and it can be difficult to pin their mood on personal issues (spousal argument, discovery of infertility, Fashion Bug out of a certain purple sweater in the correct size, etc.) or professional ones. Since the Office Girls are sweet and fun to work with, they can sometimes be mistaken for possessing a somewhat cavalier attitude toward boring administrative tasks. If you do a little too much whining in their presence or manage to avoid the actual act of working with too much success, they will not hesitate to crack the whip.

The Office Girls also function as gatekeepers to the boss. They present a formidable barrier to those seeking contact with senior management, and to this end it may prove worthwhile to curry the Office Girls' favor (flowers usually do the trick). Those unfortunate enough to land on the gatekeeper's shit list should brace themselves for repeated utterance of the sentence "He's in a meeting" and should expect to be placed on hold indefinitely. Crafty managers realize that by bestowing upon an Office Girl even the slightest hint of appreciation, they are gaining a lifelong ally. The Office Girls are so desperate for positive reinforcement that they will happily go out of their way to stuff envelopes on deadline for supervisors who treat them like fellow human beings.

MEMORABLE QUOTES

◆ "My nephews are visiting for the weekend. I can't wait!"

◆ *"My Big Fat Greek Wedding* was such a good movie."

◆ "I was in at six this morning finishing Peter's holiday itinerary."

THE OFFICE MANAGER

Within the office proper exists a cult of power more cliquey than the Office Girls, more mysterious (if less well paid) than the Consultants, and more useless than most Temps. We refer, of course, to the glorified Office Depot clerks who call the supply closet home. Fulfilling a position of which the major requirements are a pulse and a bad attitude, the Office Manager inhabits a realm completely unrelated to whatever services the company provides. Though she has absolutely no grasp on the type of work done in the office, the Office Manager professes to know exactly how you should be doing your job. When not ordering copy paper, she enjoys reprimanding you for wearing an earring (if you're male) and enforcing esoteric policies of her own creation (like the time you needed a paper clip at a quarter after one and she told you the supply closet was open only from ten till noon and two to four even though she was standing right there).

In this day and age, when anyone can grab the Staples catalog and order supplies to his or her heart's content, many offices have weaned themselves from dependence on an Office Manager. Those who do remain employed find themselves responsible for a wide assortment of responsibilities not necessarily suggested by a quick glance at the organizational flowchart. In addition to rationing Post-its, these Office Managers are in charge of such things as the phone bill (make too many long-distance calls and you'll call down their wrath), the reconciliation of time sheets, and the über-important organization of "special" days and events, such as Dress Down Fridays, Potluck Lunch Day, and all off-site meetings. The Office Manager's master plans are communicated to the office through carefully worded mass e-mail messages, which take her the better part of the day to write. Making use of such techniques as mixed fonts (for effect), alternating color, embedded art objects, and related Web links, these e-mail notices require the full engagement of the Office Manager's brainpower and usually close with one final flourish: the deployment of the autosignature option, allowing her to sign off in cursive.

Since the supply closet is often situated in some awkward, out-of-the-way nook or cranny, the Office Manager must be able to adapt successfully to a physically unorthodox workspace. Like mountain goats, after years on the job the Office Manager considers it second nature to toil in an environment boasting much greater vertical space than horizontal. It is for this reason that most employees find themselves stumbling about in a drunken haze any time they dare enter the supply closet to find something on their own. Of course, most Office Managers strictly forbid such forays into their terrain. They are more territorial than a new girlfriend at a high school reunion.

Due to the current craze for downsizing, the duties of a recently relieved Office Manager often fall to the main Receptionist, who instantly shifts from the perkiest member of the staff to a frustrated and embittered woman unable to cease from muttering the refrain "This wasn't in my goddamn job description." However, rather than trigger an ad hoc, "take whatever you want" attitude, these de facto Office Managers tend to grow frugal to the point of insanity. They hate that they're now responsible for the office supplies yet cling to them as if they're childhood mementos.

The Office Manager is, above all things, a good housekeeper. Even in offices where the staff is free to get their own supplies, she is responsible for keeping things stocked and orderly. She is the glue that holds the office together, albeit a

black coffee–swilling, chain-smoking glue that barks commands out of the side of its mouth. In order to appear super
busy, the Office Manager studiously adopts an annoyed appearance and remains in constant motion. Catch her if you can.

MEMORABLE QUOTES

◆ "I'm going to need you to fill out the proper paperwork for
those Post-its."

◆ "I'm sure I don't have to remind you that these supplies are
for office use only."

◆ "Legal size? You can't use letter? [Sigh.] You're gonna need to
give me some time on that. Special requests require notice.
This isn't a convenience store."

PERFORMANCE REVIEW AND DEVELOPMENT REPORT

Employee: The Overqualified Foreign Receptionist

> **Only the most significant and important points need to be recorded as a reference for the next review.**

The Overqualified Foreign Receptionist possesses a master's degree in applied biochemistry and had set her sights on medical school before ultimately opting in favor of emigration. Fortunately for upper management, her advanced degrees and impressive on-site experience are thoroughly meaningless in the American economy. Due to some snafu or cultural ambiguity (no doubt relating to the unstable conditions of her motherland), her transcript translates to the United States less smoothly than does her ability to keep a calendar. Unable to capitalize on her accomplishments, the Foreign Receptionist is forced to start over from scratch.

And so the Pompous General Partner's phone is now answered (and his kitchen sink now scrubbed) by an individual whose own intelligence, ambition, and talent thoroughly dwarf his own. The Foreign Receptionist is marginalized due primarily to her "cute" accent and "endearing" unfamiliarity with American customs. Coworkers who actually take the time to get to know her are struck by both the astuteness of her observations (she possesses the rare ability to describe succinctly the various ways she despises her job) and the breadth of her curiosity, though most remain primarily impressed by her mastery of the dishwasher.

Additionally, the Foreign Receptionist is engaged in some esoteric field of postgraduate study or other, a pursuit that sounds as if it should take her no more than the better part of a decade to complete. Companies engaged heavily in overseas business transactions employ the Foreign Receptionist in order to lend themselves a heightened air of legitimacy. That is, a firm in the business of exploiting, say, the Polish economy can easily impress prospective foreign clients simply by recruiting a woman with a Polish accent to man the telephones.

Comments and Recommendations: Destined either to take control of the company once her degree is completed or settle down with some random American guy to score a green card.

PERFORMANCE REVIEW AND DEVELOPMENT REPORT

Employee: The Politico

> **Only the most significant and important points need to be recorded as a reference for the next review.**

Suffering from the delusion that his drab workstation represents the dignified confines of a political think tank, the Politico spends the majority of his day attempting to enlighten his lazy, nonactivist coworkers and is the greatest flooder of e-mail inboxes since Viagra hit the black market. Most officemates spend upwards of an hour and a half daily deleting his electronic communiqués.

Largely incapable of original thought, he is little more than a forwarder of postings authored by political activist groups and Web sites. Liberal Politicos feverishly obey the commands of such anti-war groups as United for Peace and Justice (UFPJ), which organizes protests and marches (broadcast via their "Calls to Action" page), as well as the superpopular MoveOn.org, which goes so far as to write templates for petition drives, thus rendering political activism a completely brain-dead activity. Conservative Politicos are no less fanatical, though seem more intrigued by watchdog groups such as Brent Bozell's Media Research Center and shower coworkers with cyberalerts lambasting CBS for having the audacity to describe Howard Dean as a centrist rather than a bed-wetting liberal.

When drafting their own missives (a rare occurrence), liberals bash the president regardless of pertinence to the issue at hand (readers from the future might easily suppose that we lived in a time of complete chaos and anarchy), while conservatives illustrate the fallacy of Democratic programs through nursery rhymes and simplistic math problems.

The Politico seems to have taken the slogan "Think Globally, Act Locally" to heart, and thus coworkers are routinely guilted into spending their weekends painting the interior of some inner-city high school or donating blood. Sometimes referred to as "Helpy Helperton," the Politico delights in noting when anyone dares ingest an animal product in the cafeteria and will rant on issues of race, class, or gender inequalities at the slightest provocation.

Comments and Recommendations: More likely to spend six months handcuffed to a tree in Oregon than be promoted.

There are people who are terrible to work with, and then there is the Pompous General Partner, a man who, despite possessing the emotional makeup of a cranky three-year-old, holds your financial well-being in his sweaty little fists. This is a man who forces his Administrative Assistant to serve him coffee at his desk, who receives faxes while vacationing, who decorates his office with garishly overblown paintings just this side (taste-wise) of a velvet Elvis, and who throws full-blown tantrums over the slightest (and most insignificant) errors in his telephone messages. These tantrums usually play out as follows:

1. A guttural, feverish bellowing emanates from the bowels of the PGP's office.

2. The PGP appears in the office proper, sweating and disoriented.

3. The PGP begins to pace back and forth while maniacally waving a crumpled telephone message above his head.

4. The PGP zeros in on whoever took the message and proceeds to verbally abuse him or her in the loudest voice possible.

5. The PGP, exasperated and hoarse, proceeds to stomp the ground with his Italian loafers while swearing or speaking in tongues.

6. The PGP, believing he has made his point, huffs and puffs his way back into his office, loudly slamming the door behind him.

The Pompous General Partner is engaged in a business that contributes absolutely nothing of worth to society. He does not produce a good or provide a service, but merely accrues wealth for wealth's own sake (for this reason, he is usually found in financial investment institutions). The man represents nothing more than a walking (or sometimes chauffeured) bottom line. He is a pillager, a plunderer, a capitalist. He reads marketing reports instead of novels and commands his wife to remain silent throughout the duration of CNN's *In the Money*. To create an illusion of humanity, the Pompous General Partner might pledge his support to some charity or worthy cause. Do not be fooled. Though of course it's just wonderful that a disadvantaged entity is indeed benefiting from the Pompous General Partner's largesse, his goodwill is obscured both by his habit of loudly and "offhandedly" mentioning his charity work, as well as by his accountant's palpable glee at the scenario's tax write-off implications.

The Pompous General Partner is often a member of a family legacy. Odds are, his father founded the corporation (or at least made some major inroads in the corporate sector) and continues to weigh in on professional matters from the lush confines of pampered semiretirement. Lesser employees are often required to entertain phone calls from the Pompous General Partner, Senior, as if they are speaking with the Queen Mother. In turn, the Pompous General Partner sires his own brood of overindulged offspring. Raised largely by live-in nannies, these children's talents are usually obscured by the benefits of their birthright. That is, while many are quite intelligent and accomplished, they really need not be; there is a slot at an Ivy League school being kept warm for them and a nice trust fund ready to kick in as soon as they come of age. To the Pompous General Partner, these children are a source of pride practically on par with his collection of beautiful silk ties.

Their most important function is an ability to appear adorable on annual holiday cards (lovingly sealed, stamped, and mailed personally by the Pompous General Partner's executive assistant).

Remember that time you skipped lunch, then stayed late in order to ensure that a certain presentation was executed perfectly? Well, neither does the Pompous General Partner. There is no skill you can master, no amount of intelligence you can offer, no dedication you can display that will impress him. He has no emotional attachment to you whatsoever. You might as well be the copy machine. Bumble the intricacies of his daily sushi order just once and you might as well pack your bags.

The Pompous General Partner is drawn to money like bar mitzvah guests to the buffet. He is single-minded and unswerving and possesses an insatiable fiduciary appetite. The monotony of this money lust leaves the Pompous General Partner with little intellectual curiosity. He is an unbelievable bore at dinner parties, and people skills are conspicuously lacking from his repertoire (HR departments exist for a reason, after all).

Of course, this doesn't mean he excels at delegation, either. The Pompous General Partner likes to get his beak wet and will often rely on New Agey substitutes for actual cognitive activity, such as subjecting prospective hires to standardized psychological evaluations (such as the woefully simplistic Caliper Profile Evaluation). The intellectual equivalent of tarot cards, such tests allow the Pompous General Partner to appear progressive while saving himself the inconvenience of say, conducting an actual interview.

Generally speaking (as it were), the Pompous General Partner gives off the air of an aging collegiate track star, which he actually is. While no longer able to impress by running briskly around an oval track, he remains quite virile for a man his age (just ask his mistress). The only real physical proof of the

Pompous General Partner's inability to resist the aging process is the slow but steady muddying of his skin tone. With a face like a bulb in the red-light district, he appears to be mere months away from dropping dead of a heart attack in his office.

MEMORABLE QUOTES

◆ "How the hell can you *not* get an e-mail address? Jesus Christ!"

◆ "Book the Harvard Club for the holiday party."

◆ "Tell my mother to hold."

PERFORMANCE REVIEW AND DEVELOPMENT REPORT

Employee: <u>The Porno Purveyor</u>

> **Only the most significant and important points need to be recorded as a reference for the next review.**

No firewall, reprimand, or raised eyebrow can stop the Porno Purveyor from completing his mission: the successful dissemination of electronic pornography to a network of supposedly like-minded male officemates. Be it Paris Hilton's slipped nipple, the Brazilian Women's Soccer Team's nude fund-raising calendar, or obviously Photoshopped shots of Anna Kournikova sunbathing in the altogether, the Porno Purveyor is a reliable source of X-rated e-mail correspondence.

The Porno Purveyor thoughtfully alerts recipients to the contents of his missives through savvy use of the Subject line. Often proceeded by an excited come-on along the lines of "This is awesome!!!!!," his cautionary advice-giving is as thrifty as it is effective ("Careful," "Beware," or "Take heed" usually suffice).

It seems possible that the Porno Purveyor is more interested in asserting his own masculinity than in ogling naked breasts. There is a certain "Look what I found!" element to his endeavors, and, furthermore, those on the receiving end of his material feel pressure to acquiesce as to the hotness of the subject matter whether or not pornography happens to be their cup of tea.

How the resident Porno Purveyor's actions do not constitute a violation of the company handbook is anybody's guess, but most are only reprimanded or terminated if the material accidentally reaches an e-mail address outside the office or if a female employee catches sight of their handiwork and claims offense to upper management.

Comments and Recommendations: Enjoys wonderful career prospects, due mainly to his supervisor's fascination with Brazilian waxing.

THE POTENTIAL SERIAL KILLER

It's quiet. Perhaps a bit too quiet. The air is crisp and still, like the surface of the moon or that time you snuck into a cemetery with your high school girlfriend after listening to too many Cure songs. You try focusing on the computer screen, taking solace in the monotonous, endless lines of pulsating digits. But something seems amiss. The hair on the back of your neck is standing at attention. Against all your better instincts, you swivel in your chair to have a look behind you.

There, in the far corner of your two-person cubicle, the Potential Serial Killer sits sharpening the point of a No. 2 pencil over and over and over again. The monotony of his movements, the scratching of wood against metal, the way he hunches over like a jeweler looking for flaws in a precious stone . . . he's really creeping you out. He looks up at you, his beady eyes betraying years of bottled-up aggression. He's perspiring and breathing somewhat heavily. Maybe you'll swing by HR on your lunch break to look into that departmental transfer you've been thinking about.

The Potential Serial Killer is a nervous, paranoid, coffee-swilling grunt. He requires twenty hours of unpaid overtime to complete tasks easy enough for most Interns to knock off before noon. Discounting a constant stream of barely audible mumblings, he speaks to no one throughout the course of the day, with the glaring exception of his mother, who telephones every half hour or so (he lives in her basement). Due to his ability to frighten his coworkers out of their wits, the Potential Serial Killer is given an extremely large berth and, excepting you (his cube-mate), occupies what amounts to his own private wing of the office. Even his supervisor hesitates to make contact and will usually force some hapless underling (e.g., the resident Temp) to approach the Potential Serial Killer and ascertain the progress of the simple report he's been working on for the last eight days.

While most sane employees would revel in the amount of freedom and real estate conferred upon the PSK, he is too wound up in his own tortured interior monologue to so much as notice the twenty-foot buffer zone vigilantly maintained by his coworkers. In addition to his aforementioned mumblings, he has been known to suffer from fits of semiviolent nervous twitching and regularly barks at you to turn your music down (even when you're wearing headphones).

The Potential Serial Killer is never without his disgustingly chewed-on Styrofoam coffee cup, from which he somehow manages to drink despite his constant case of the shakes. In the six years you've been with the company (fourteen less than he), the Potential Serial Killer has not paid one visit to the cafeteria or gone out for lunch. Instead, he opts to eat at his desk from a brown paper sack rolled and *stapled* shut. The menu does not vary: peanut butter (creamy) on white bread, no crust, and a solitary bruised pear. All washed down, of course, with his thirtieth cup of coffee.

There are but two occasions when the Potential Serial Killer rises from his seat and leaves his desk (not counting midnight, when he finally heads home): to refill his coffee in the kitchen and to relieve himself in the men's room. These journeys represent the lone occasions on which most of the staff come in contact with him, and those seated along his route have been known to shudder as he passes behind them. Because he doesn't raise his feet when he walks, the Potential Serial Killer can be heard shuffling toward you from a decent distance, allowing ample time to roll in as close to your desk as is humanly possible.

Due to his fear of being fired or reprimanded, the Potential Serial Killer displays a constant look of terror and tends to be incredibly jumpy. In an effort to dissuade such action from taking place, and in lieu of actual productivity, he takes great pains to impress his superiors with the Zen-like cleanliness of his workstation, which remains as free of dust and debris as it does of personal effects. Of course, the rigidity of his neatness only wigs you out further, to the point that you're absolutely convinced that he is on the verge of something unthinkable. The only evidence that someone inhabits his cubicle can be found in the (always locked) upper drawer of his desk, in which he keeps a series of densely scribbled-in composition pads. Those who are both aware of these notebooks and have seen the movie *Seven* have not failed to make the connection.

MEMORABLE QUOTES

♦ [indecipherable nervous giggling/laughter.]

♦ "I type with only my right index finger."

♦ "I once had a small dog . . ."

Employee: The Prairie Dog

> **Only the most significant and important points need to be recorded as a reference for the next review.**

Nothing gets the Prairie Dog's attention quite like the snippets of conversation heard over and through the thin walls of his cubicle. He can be sidetracked by subjects both mundane (who's going to lunch when) and reasonably intriguing (insert name of latest secretary to be inappropriately propositioned by the sleazy boss here).

The Prairie Dog registers his interest in various conversations by poking his head up over the wall of his cube with the quickness and frequency of those pop-up rodents meant to be bopped on the head in the popular arcade attraction, an action reported to startle coworkers unaccustomed to his presence. Certain nearby cube dwellers have even been known to yelp upon being greeted by the sight of the Prairie Dog's eager face perched overhead, his chin resting squarely on the upper edge of their faux office wall.

Though he will occasionally spring up silently in order to ascertain the identity of the participants and the particulars of a conversation (and to gauge his own level of interest in the proceedings), more often than not the Prairie Dog's buoyancy is accompanied by some verbal inquisition, such as "What was that?," "Did somebody say 'Coffee'?," or "You guys missed the game last night?"

The Prairie Dog is so closely associated with this character trait that most employees are unable to recognize him outside the context of his seemingly disembodied head. His body type is virtually unknown, as is his preferred style of dress. On occasion, he will be eyed suspiciously at a company picnic or barbecue by coworkers convinced that he has crashed the affair.

Comments and Recommendations: Claims to have recently overheard rumor of his own promotion drifting over from some cubicle due south of his.

PERFORMANCE REVIEW AND DEVELOPMENT REPORT

Employee: The Prodigal Son

> **Only the most significant and important points need to be recorded as a reference for the next review.**

Fresh off a six-month stint backpacking through Europe, the Prodigal Son has returned to take his rightful place on the fast track to corporate inheritance. Despite possessing neither interest in nor affinity for the business at hand, the Prodigal Son is by birthright entitled to assume the reins just as soon as his middle-aged father (the president and CEO) decides to step aside.

He is OK with clients and seems to possess a basic understanding of the telephone. People skills are not his strong suit, though he does quite well with the secretarial pool. Passed-over middle managers seem reluctant to accept the Prodigal Son into the fold, though the CEO encourages them to make him feel welcome while they've still got jobs.

His father expresses both disgust over his inability to focus on anything not related to the acquisition and playback of bootlegged jam band recordings and a pathetic determination that the boy simply "learn the ropes" and "get involved."

The Prodigal Son can be moody and a bit of a tyrant. He grows visibly bored when confronted with official business and naps at shareholders' meetings. He regularly sends his administrative staff out on shopping excursions of a personal nature and recently elected to chastise his most senior assistant for failing to book the particular ski chalet he had requested. There is no recourse for those bearing the brunt of his naïveté, save resignation or performing the Prodigal Son's work for him without hope of compensation.

If the Prodigal Son continues to shirk responsibility, the CEO has vowed that his younger brother, Chad, will ascend the throne in his place . . . a hollow threat that seems unlikely at best, given Chad's predilection for musical theater.

Comments and Recommendations: Barring some unforeseen, scandalous episode involving his father's male valet and a French maid's outfit, it should prove virtually impossible for him *not* to advance swiftly.

You've finally made your move. After years of toil, working your fingers to the bone, groveling before your corporate masters, you've given your notice. Two more weeks of slacking off, and you're out of here. All that remains are a few e-mail messages, a couple of drawers to clean out, some halfhearted promises to "keep in touch." But wait. What's this? No, it cannot be. They wouldn't dare. Welcome to your worst nightmare: the Protégée has arrived.

Oh, she acts so sweet and innocent. So eager. But don't be fooled; the Protégée is a diabolical creature and exists only to make your life a living hell. The comfort zone you've spent years cultivating is about to be blown to smithereens. Your cubicle, barely large enough to house one humanely, is now going to be shared. The Protégée will peer over your shoulder like a parrot. There is no keystroke of which she won't make note, no phone conversation to which she will not be privy. And you might as well forget all about Instant Messenger; those days are over.

The Protégée's overeagerness makes her appear childlike and easily flustered. Though perhaps secretly competent, she is confounded by tasks and operating procedures most toddlers could grasp instantly. How the Protégée made it past the interview stage is anybody's guess. Perhaps a slow day down at HR. Or, more likely, the boss panicked and jumped to hire someone, anyone, to replace you. At any rate, here she is; all dressed up in her shiny shoes and ill-fitting suit and ready to work. And guess who has to train her.

What's most infuriating about the Protégée is that this isn't really her fault. It's a question of personal space. There's nowhere to run, no way to get away from each other. It's like waking up one morning to find you've got a Siamese twin. For her part, the Protégée approaches the situation with treacly kindness and goodwill. It is common for her to show up for work bearing little gifts: home-baked cookies, brownies, other sweets, or, also popular, delectable ethnic leftovers from last night's dinner. She is a master of food-based emotional blackmail.

The Protégée seems completely incapable of grasping that her mere presence is a source of nuisance. To make matters worse, she never stops talking. Not ever. Hers is an incessant stream of mundane dialogue peppered with preposterously easy-to-figure-out questions. Her queries simply will not cease. It's like the Spanish Inquisition minus the accent. She is not discouraged by the sight of headphones, rolled eyes, or pained expressions. The barrage will continue despite your best efforts.

The Protégée is slow to make friends and usually sticks to those unlucky enough to be assigned to her. There are few sights more depressing than the Protégée eating lunch alone in a far corner of the cafeteria, hunched over some lurid mass market paperback. She's not exactly a pariah, but her newness makes her something of an oddity. Furthermore, her eagerness is a stark counterpoint to the soul-dead, beaten-down personalities of those around her. It's even rumored that she actually enjoys working. Of course, her humanity will ultimately be trampled by the job, but until then most coworkers will continue to shy away from her. She's too bouncy, too not miserable. But give her a few weeks.

MEMORABLE QUOTES

◆ "Do you like sugar cookies? I made these last night. Here, have some."

◆ "How do I restart the computer?"

◆ "What's the copier code again?"

PERFORMANCE REVIEW AND DEVELOPMENT REPORT

Employee: The Proximity Crush

> **Only the most significant and important points need to be recorded as a reference for the next review.**

The Proximity Crush is working out quite well. She seems to have accrued some valuable experience at her various internships, and she exhibits a nuanced, well-thought-out approach to her duties unusual for someone only six months out of college. Her computer skills are excellent, and she appears to be genuinely interested in succeeding both for her own sake and for the company's.

Plus, she's unbelievably adorable. That sky blue sweater set she pranced about in last Wednesday was particularly breathtaking, even better than the time she leaned over to check a scratch on the photocopier's glass wearing those skintight black slacks that drive her male coworkers wild. Her skill set is so highly valued that her immediate supervisors display a tendency to vie publicly for her assistance.

Mr. Naughton in Accounting recently hip-checked Mr. O'Grady from Legal when each found the other striding purposely toward the Proximity Crush's cubicle, cologne freshly applied and busywork in hand. Exit interviews with each suggest an inability to focus when in the Proximity Crush's presence, yet a complete inability to recall her existence post five p.m. In addition, all young male employees within twenty yards of her workstation regularly feign incompetence in order to request the Proximity Crush's assistance. They too find her spellbindingly appealing while at the office yet lose track of her allure once in the company of their girlfriends or drinking buddies.

The Proximity Crush remains completely unaware of her on-site charm and in fact seems a bit lonely. She has recently begun snacking on bonbons at her desk and claims to adore both *When Harry Met Sally* and *Sleepless in Seattle.*

Comments and Recommendations: If she can manage to avoid the aging process, her prospects are limitless.

The Recently Downsized, Overeager New Hire should have just stayed retired. Let's face it: he's not getting any younger, corporate culture is changing all around him, and he's already given his best years to an industry that barely noted his contributions. The kids are out of college, the house is paid off, his wife claims to find him attractive still. It's about time he learned to relax and enjoy himself.

Unfortunately for his ego, however, his day of professional reckoning arrived slightly sooner than he'd planned. Sure, he could head off into the sunset, but he wants to leave on his own terms. Severance package be damned, he's not about to be downsized quietly. He'll show those bastards. And so several months pass, months spent unshaven and brooding around the house, calling headhunters, posting résumés online. After the first week, his wife is pulling her hair out. He enjoys golf and the morning paper and . . . he can't quite remember *what* he enjoys. What do people do all day? It's been thirty years since his life didn't revolve around the office. Time to get back to work, to the only lifestyle he knows.

Despite advancing age (and receding hair), the Recently Downsized, Overeager New Hire gets a break. He's hired for an executive position at a small, progressive firm. A firm that for all intents and purposes is already thriving, just raking in the cash. Everyone's happy and getting richer. The General Partner, while Pompous, is something of a visionary in the field. This is cutting-edge stuff; this office is a well-oiled machine. But the RD, O New Hire needs to establish himself and make his presence felt. The nice new corner office isn't sending the message strongly enough. He's going to blaze a trail and think outside the box, yet still make certain to dot every *i* and cross every *t*. He's going to show these people just what he's made of and just how indispensable he is. He's going to obsessively alter their already flawless sales material until it reflects his own ingenuity. He's going to cut quite an impressive figure, never mind the paunch. Occasionally, the Pompous General Partner will cut the Recently Downsized, Overeager New Hire down to size (pun intended), though the latter usually responds by sulking back to his office in order to work on rephrasing his initial request in a new light.

Somewhere in the office there's an executive assistant whose life is about to become a living hell. Never again will she take a lunch break, check her e-mail, or leave her desk (save for brief excursions to the restroom). The RD, O New Hire is going to work her like a mule or a copy machine. After all, he's an idea man; he doesn't do the dirty work. It's not that his ideas are all that horrible, just completely unnecessary. The RD, O New Hire is the law of diminishing returns personified. Yes, after six weeks of paranoid delusional instruction and back-breaking effort, that PowerPoint presentation he decided to "jazz up" may indeed boast a few more colorful details, but it's still essentially unchanged after going through more revisions than the galleys of *Infinite Jest*. And just try explaining to the RD, O New Hire the benefits of converting the file to Adobe Acrobat. It's like lecturing your new puppy on the finer points of the stem cell research debate.

The Recently Downsized, Overeager New Hire is like a one-man executive assistant furlough program. The most sweet-natured of assistants find the position unbearable after several months, and even those with three or four high-maintenance young children at home consider the RD, O New Hire's constant need for assistance to be a bit much to take. Still, someone is destined for this drudgery, if only for a few weeks. Hopefully, it's not you.

MEMORABLE QUOTES

◆ "This presentation looks great, but I'm wondering if we can't use a slightly larger font for my name. Could you look into that?"

◆ "Can you come in here and show me how to use my e-mail again?"

◆ "I understand how the lunch has always been ordered. I'd just like to try out a new system."

Anyone with a winning lottery ticket and an extended family knows just how overwhelming a constantly ringing telephone can be. Multiply this by about five billion and you'll have some idea of the Receptionist's daily plight. Since most office folk consider the simple process of lifting a receiver to their ear and saying "Hello" a Herculean task on par with, say, competing in the Ironman Triathlon or getting in on time, the Receptionist must toil as middleman between caller and callee. Many offices do not even allow calls to be placed directly, and so each communiqué must flow through the front desk, where the Receptionist handles the switchboard with a flurry of movement broken only by the periodic flipping of the pages of her *Cosmo*.

In a setting where workers pursue career advancement like salmon swimming upstream to mate, the Receptionist is a stagnant anomaly. Make no mistake: she's going nowhere (save eventual retirement). Excepting a possible promotion to secretary, most Receptionists treat the position as a permanent one. This is their life's work, which you might want to bear in mind the next time you order her to clean up after the lunch meeting you've just attended. But then again, corporate maid is often an official aspect of the Receptionist's job description, so don't feel too bad. It is quite common for her to spend as much time cleansing the kitchen sink as scribbling messages.

Receptionists are overwhelmingly female. Why exactly this is isn't completely clear (as it's been quite a while, after all, since women were discouraged from pursuing nonsecretarial careers), but the position is so closely associated with females that male Receptionists are routinely regarded as homosexual. At any rate, the job is fairly straightforward: answer the phones, take messages, deal with visitors, order kitchen supplies, loan out umbrellas, make copies, schedule conference rooms, etc. This isn't the most taxing (or interesting) position in the world, and most Receptionists are thoroughly interchangeable. What is interesting, if not the position itself, is the cast of characters most likely to fill it. These are the people you're most likely to first encounter while traipsing in late:

1. *The Baby Momma.* This independent, single mother is just trying to support her baby after her no good daddy just up and left. You've no doubt admired her baby photos (one for each season, plus one in mini basketball gear) and commiserated over her lack of child support.

2. *The Coulda-Been-a-Librarian.* This middle-aged, corn-fed Receptionist is beginning to fill out a bit around the middle (an observation you've tried really hard not to verbalize). She is always pleasant, always on time, and answers the phone as if it's the best thing that ever happened to her. You have feigned interest in her annual trip to the Midwest to visit her sister or cousin (you can't recall which).

3. *The Serial Chatterer.* Pity all those who call the office while the Serial Chatterer is manning the phones. She will gab with anyone on any topic, though her favorites include the weather, Jewish holidays, and the flu. The Serial Chatterer spends an average of twelve minutes on the line with each caller and ignores the flashing red lights of other incoming calls until she is quite through.

4. *The Cute-but-Dumb.* Not quite intelligent enough to hold down a job at McDonald's, the Cute-but-Dumb Receptionist needs to be retrained on the phone and computer systems each time she returns from vacation. She is so cute and perky, however, that upper management is more than willing to overlook her incompetence.

5. *The Unofficially Tenured.* This Receptionist has been with the company for at least fifty years and no one has the heart to fire her. She is noted more for the wide assortment of candy in her glass dish than for filling any actual professional function. Just passing her in the corridor reminds you that it's been a while since you called your grandmother.

6. *The Girl Screwing the Boss.* Whether or not this Receptionist is actually screwing the boss is anybody's guess, but to the assembled staff her ridiculously short skirt is evidence enough. Also fuel for thought: her willingness to laugh heartily at every bad pun–filled joke flung her way by her superior.

7. *The Former Dot-Commer.* The most common male Receptionist, the Former Dot-Commer once pulled down six figures, but this was the only position he could find after his severance package ran out. He wears a headset that makes him look like an Old Navy floor boy and reads *Wired* incessantly. He is your main competition for the affections of the cute girl in Accounting.

Regardless of which Receptionist calls your office home, her presence there affords what is no doubt a refreshing respite from the career-driven automatons around you. After all, who else initiates spirited debates concerning Erica Kane's taste in men and actually telephones the help desk to address problems with her computerized Solitaire?

MEMORABLE QUOTES

◆ "The boss was looking for you, but don't worry . . . I told him you're never in before ten."

◆ "Can you watch the phones while I get my hair done?"

◆ "Where's your green for St. Patrick's Day?"

PERFORMANCE REVIEW AND DEVELOPMENT REPORT

Employee: The Sappy Matron

> **Only the most significant and important points need to be recorded as a reference for the next review.**

A walking baby factory, the Sappy Matron's three to five purportedly adorable young children have done little to quell her taste for all things juvenile, sophomoric, or traditional. Her cubicle is draped in baby photos and supposedly inspirational posters of puppies and kittens ("Hang in there!"), all of which lend her workstation the appearance of a Hallmark store (which, incidentally, ranks right up there with the Christmas Tree Shop as her favorite place to hang out).

The Sappy Matron is the office's lowest common denominator. She adores mainstream, unchallenging fare and dreams of one day visiting the Mall of America or perhaps, if she's feeling crazy, taking a Disney cruise. She is empathetic in the extreme and regularly interrupts her own secretarial work in order to soothe some whimpering coworker who's just been dumped, reprimanded, or diagnosed with carpal tunnel.

She is an avowed teetotaler and thus eschews happy hour in order to rush home, watch the kids, and prepare her husband's dinner (most likely a five-plate smorgasbord of Americana involving some combination of baked ham, macaroni and cheese, meatloaf, green beans, and Crescent Rolls). Certain coworkers do, however, claim to have witnessed her sipping the alcoholic eggnog at last season's holiday party, though she was likely just trying not to hurt anyone's feelings.

The Sappy Matron's hairstyle, wardrobe, and musical tastes are all a good ten years out of date. Fellow employees who come in contact with the Sappy Matron find that she seems "nice enough" yet come away from the encounter vowing never to settle down or have children.

Comments and Recommendations: Give her another year and she'll be working part-time at a florist and volunteering with the PTA.

PERFORMANCE REVIEW AND DEVELOPMENT REPORT

Employee: The Scavenger

> **Only the most significant and important points need to be recorded as a reference for the next review.**

With an appetite that eclipses even the Vulture's culinary trespasses, the Scavenger's sole function is the accumulation of things that do not belong to her. She will stop at nothing to hoard an entire apartment full of highly sought-after objects (CDs, video games, books, etc.).

The Scavenger refers to the fruit of her five-finger discount as "swag" and considers the haul to represent a reasonable perk of her lowly station, particularly given the paltry compensation she receives for performing a variety of low-level administrative tasks (answering the telephone, stuffing envelopes, ordering lunch, dog-sitting her boss's designer pooch). She excels when employed by a magazine or other such entity where products are provided free of charge in hopes of review or other mention.

The Scavenger is the envy of her friends, the majority of whom express disdain over the fact that the best stuff they've ever stolen from the office was a lifetime supply of Post-its and an admittedly handy roll of packing tape. Since her official function seems less than likely to result in any significant promotions, her supervisors choose to ignore the Scavenger's wild-eyed pocketing of goods to keep her distracted from the fact that she's going nowhere fast.

Like a housewife in Atlantic City, the Scavenger sometimes gets "the fever" and becomes unable to differentiate between promotional materials and, say, that crystal frog one-year-anniversary present her coworker Nancy temporarily placed on their shared cubicle wall.

Comments and Recommendations: A decent worker who should advance smoothly (though slowly) unless caught rifling through the contents of her superior's handbag.

THE SECURITY GUARD

The Security Guard is like a doorman at a bar where nobody would ever want to hang out. In a building where all anyone can think of is the moment they get to leave, he judiciously stands watch over those who enter. If the Security Guard really wanted to do some good, he'd screen people on their way *out* in order to thwart plans of three-hour lunches and weekend head starts. But as it is, he'll feebly request that you sign in or absentmindedly avert his eyes from the sports page long enough to cast a fleeting glance in the general direction of your ID card. The Security Guard is more lax than a Jersey Shore bouncer; you can flash a lottery scratch card and be waved toward the elevators.

However, in this age of heightened security measures, certain office buildings have begun vigilantly screening all who enter. Security Guards posted at such locales have hit the power trip jackpot. Gaining entrance to Pfizer headquarters in New York City, for example, can be more difficult than ascending to the top floor of a Masonic temple. Someone must really be after that secret Viagra formula, because the marble lobby is patrolled with a sense of urgency usually reserved for Scotland Yard. You haven't seen authority misapplied this egregiously since your run-in with the fifth-grade hall monitor. And God help you if you're there as a visitor. Adopting a child entails a less thorough screening process than does successfully convincing these Security Guards that your best friend works in the building.

In most cases, however, the Security Guard is content simply to sit there on his metal folding chair, sip coffee, doze off, smoke the occasional cigarette, and stare bleary-eyed at his quadrants of black-and-white video images. He doesn't want to be bothered, and fortunately for him this isn't the most mentally taxing of positions. Neither, for that matter, is it a physically taxing one. The most arduous task most Security Guards face is squeezing themselves into the uniform every morning. Offices in which employees are given an electronic ID card to pass over a sensor upon entry feature particularly lazy and disengaged Security Guards, who are essentially paid just to sit there and give the appearance of security. They've got it made.

Some Security Guards are more vigilant than others, and which kind stands watch over your office building has a great deal to do with its location. In urban environments, most companies feature the Minority Security Guard, who provides a contrast to the racial demographic of those around him. Whether or not this dynamic leads to greater security is anyone's guess, but it does provide the middle-class, mostly white employees an opportunity to try out the street slang they picked up on MTV's *Cribs*. These painfully uncool suburban office drones find it impossible to flash their ID cards without uttering something along the lines of "Yo," "What up?," or "This is where I get my job on." The Minority Security Guard usually humors such dialogue but visibly bristles at particularly over-the-top comments, such as "Sharpton seemed like a viable presidential candidate to me."

In offices further removed from a large city, the Security Guard is no doubt some unbelievable loser who couldn't quite cut it in the military (he was likely discharged for a shaky emotional state) and so is instead living out his *Rambo* fantasy in your lobby. Sporting a jarhead crew cut and suspiciously well-sculpted muscles (revealed by the obscenely rolled-up sleeves of his uniform), this Security Guard wields his clipboard like an Uzi, never takes his shades off, and refers to *Heartbreak*

Ridge as "the greatest movie ever made." Don't get in this guy's way; he will break you faster than a sexual harassment review board. If he says he can't read your signature, write it neater; if he makes an off-color joke concerning "those goddamn A-rabs" or "gays," just chuckle; if he asks what type of car you drive, say something American. Due to his unenlightened demeanor and brute physical strength, this guy usually does quite well with the Cute-but-Dumb Receptionist. He will routinely concoct some type of "breach" with the Receptionist's ID card in order to flirt a little longer.

You never know when you might require the Security Guard's assistance with, say, the receipt of a personal delivery. So it's best to keep him on your good side. Always smile, act courteous, and inquire as to the quality of his day. Take an interest in your Security Guard. High-five him when appropriate.

MEMORABLE QUOTES

◆ "You can't wheel that dolly through the front entrance, pal."

◆ "Sixteenth floor. I think."

◆ "Eh, you don't need to sign in if you don't feel like it."

THE SHOCKINGLY INCOMPETENT AUTHORITY FIGURE

Hairstyle lifted from favorite women's studies professor

Totally just lost her train of thought

Pirate clown blouse wards off respect

"Maybe this part should be in italics?" (As if that's the problem)

Commute shoes

The Friday-morning deadline looms. There are important people waiting; professional reputations are at stake. According to normal protocol, you'll just need to look over your superior's work, perhaps brighten a few details, then pass it along. No big deal; it'll be happy hour before you know it. But now it's Thursday, three p.m., and you still haven't seen anything. What's taking her so long? You decide to kill a little time on IM. Finally, an hour later, she e-mails the document. Whew, just in time. You open the file, start reading . . . it's the biggest piece of garbage this side of your high school's poetry annual. You scan the file heading; perhaps she forwarded her third-grader's English homework by mistake? No such luck. This thing reads worse than chick lit.

Welcome to life under the Shockingly Incompetent Authority Figure. How someone with a BA in cartography ever wound up managing a large investment bank's retirement plan services is anybody's guess, but what's clear is that your teenage babysitting gig is turning out to be more professionally useful than the six years you wasted studying finance. No house full of screaming babes came close to approaching your office's consistently frantic feel. The Shockingly Incompetent Authority Figure enjoys burdening her assistants with a litany of concurrent projects and busywork she will never actually utilize (nice job on those organizational flowcharts, though). Moreover, all work, regardless of difficulty or import, is performed only at the very last possible moment, often by more than one person, each of whom, unbeknownst to the other, was assigned the identical task by the SIAF during a particularly absentminded attempt at supervision. Her assistants spend more time picking up the pieces than they do getting anything accomplished.

Of course, the Shockingly Incompetent Authority Figure believes that she is in fact incredibly competent and quite an effective role model to her young charges. She has no sense that her lack of social skills makes her particularly ill equipped to communicate with underlings and remains ignorant of her inability to delegate or to differentiate between employees of varying skill level. The Shockingly Incompetent Authority Figure thinks nothing of asking you to wash out her coffee mug just as soon as you've finished drafting that priority report for the Board of Directors.

Since a glaring lack of real-world experience is a mainstay of her general ineptitude, the Shockingly Incompetent Authority Figure feels most at home in academic settings, where one may wile away the years free from the burden of actual professional responsibility (save for perhaps occasional pressure to publish some obscure article nobody will ever read). But of course she knows no such bounds and will work anywhere, regardless of industry. Wherever time, effort, and paper can be wasted, the Shockingly Incompetent Authority Figure may be found. Outsiders (that is, anyone who doesn't work directly under her) actually think she's doing a great job, which really makes your blood boil as you attempt, once again, to show her how to access the database.

The Shockingly Incompetent Authority Figure has two sure-fire methods for pulling the wool over the office's eyes. The first requires her to do little more than consistently flatter and flirt with both her boss and one highly skilled employee on her own level. The occasional hotel room tryst doesn't hurt either, a move the Shockingly Incompetent Authority Figure will resort to as necessary (wedding rings notwithstanding). The boss enjoys the boon to his virility so much that he'll keep her around at any cost, while the highly skilled coworker (who's most likely stuck in a crumbling marriage) doesn't mind bailing her out in a pinch as long she keeps telling him it looks like he's lost weight.

Her second method is at once more diabolical and more successful, though it does require the SIAF to possess some talent. All that is required is that she perform some feat directly out of college (coining some groundbreaking economic theory, say) that blows everyone away. Once this has been accomplished, the Shockingly Incompetent Authority Figure is free to install herself in the office of her choosing, piece together a staff, and proceed to slack off until retirement, coasting on the fumes of her youthful accomplishment.

Which is where you come in, since the greatest boon to the SIAF's professional longevity is her flair for hiring people who excel at remedying her blunders. Her impressive reputation effectively fools new hires into believing that they've stumbled upon an opportunity to work for someone with great experience in the field. It can take years for you to figure out that your boss is the crazy one, not you.

MEMORABLE QUOTES

◆ "Can you do me a favor and make dinner reservations, check the train schedule for my trip, draft the annual shareholders' report, drop my daughter off at school, and print out nineteen copies of my résumé by noon? Thanks."

◆ "You guys can't charge so much paper and so many paper clips to the office's account. You know we're already overbudget from the business trip I took to Cancún last month."

◆ "Oh, don't worry if you don't finish this project by the end of the day . . . You can just drive it out to my house this weekend. Oh, and on the way would you mind picking up a dresser I have in storage? Thanks so much."

Employee: The Single Pet Owner

> **Only the most significant and important points need to be recorded as a reference for the next review.**

The Single Pet Owner is the office's most pathetic employee. In addition to rolling their eyes at the latest in-depth description of her pooch's poop output, some coworkers have been known to craft increasingly vulgar sex jokes involving the Single Pet Owner and her favorite companion.

The Single Pet Owner is doomed to a spinsterlike existence due to the difficulty of finding a man who is willing to allow his life to revolve around the mundane exploits of a mangy animal. Even suitors unaccountably attracted to the Single Pet Owner are ultimately rebuffed when it becomes apparent that their commitment pales in comparison to the mindless loyalty of an indentured canine.

The Single Pet Owner operates out of a cubicle decorated with photographic depictions of animals wearing human clothing and contorted into unnatural poses (sad-looking dogs in Santa hats or reindeer ears are quite popular). Some fanatical Single Pet Owners go so far as to create a monthly calendar starring their own pets. There is no business topic that the Single Pet Owner cannot morph into an intricate rumination on the color of puke, the density (and frequency) of poop, the godsend that are wee-wee pads, the price and availability of local dog walkers, the adventure of a trip to the veterinarian, or the ranked merits of various doggie treats.

The Single Pet Owner rarely travels and thus possesses a rather limited worldview. She has been known to skip holiday travel altogether when her cat seems reluctant to fly and can entertain the notion of vacationing only in terms of how it will affect her pets. The Single Pet Owner places the comfort of her animals in higher esteem than her own and regularly arrives late to work due to her dog's tummyache.

Her life is incredibly uninteresting, and contact with the Single Pet Owner can turn otherwise humane people into avowed animal haters.

Comments and Recommendations: Her productivity wanes periodically, though a quick smack with a rolled-up newspaper usually rectifies the situation.

PERFORMANCE REVIEW AND DEVELOPMENT REPORT

Employee: The Social Organizer

> **Only the most significant and important points need to be recorded as a reference for the next review.**

The former social chair of Drexel University's Phi Kappa Sigma chapter, the Social Organizer makes it his business to ensure that the office schedules happy hours, field trips, half days, holiday parties, and other random events designed to limit productivity as often as possible. A recent college graduate, the Social Organizer is reluctant to abandon a lifestyle centered primarily on beer slinging and womanizing.

He views the office as one big party just waiting to happen and is determined to help each and every employee get his or her drink on. To further facilitate a festive atmosphere, the Social Organizer spends vast quantities of time and effort obsessing over mix CDs. Once completed, the discs are distributed to coworkers according to theme and relevance ("Data Entry Mix Vol. 1"; "Old School Filing Jams"; "Holiday Party Super Hits" [2 Disc Set]; etc.).

The Social Organizer exercises before work, and the resulting adrenaline rush tends to make him the office's most chipper personality (an effect largely extinguished by four p.m.). He has few if any enemies and acts as a fun-loving confidant to both upper management and Interns alike. His favorite conversational topics include Las Vegas, local bands, and snowboarding.

The Social Organizer is known to deejay weekend college parties, events particularly cool coworkers are invited to via Thursday afternoon Evite. When not scheduling a workplace outing, the Social Organizer busily maintains an online database intended to facilitate coordination of his impending high school reunion.

Comments and Recommendations: Wonderful prospects as long as he can avoid a tragic limbo accident at next spring's company pig roast (which he's coordinating now).

Old-lady
smell

Puts quite a drain
on company's
health insurance
provider

Frequent visits
to restroom

Swollen
feet

The office can be a lonely place, utterly devoid of warmth and humanity. Like Roman slaves, corporate work staffs toil for absurd periods of time (forty hours a week? Outrageous!), interrupted by only fleeting respite (a half-hour lunch break straight out of third grade) and made semipalatable by miserly reward (hence your new Honda Civic). In addition, the slave driver, er . . . boss, runs a tight and unimaginative ship, forcing those below him to dress according to rigid codes and make do with operating systems of a decidedly ancient vintage. It's easy, while hurriedly pecking away, gritting your teeth against carpel tunnel, to feel unloved and underappreciated. What you wouldn't give for a nice, big hug.

Fortunately, there exists among the office pool a glowing ray of sunshine just waiting to warm your soul. The Surrogate Grandmother is there for you, even if it feels a bit creepy and awkward at first. Those new to the office might be a bit disarmed by her very presence, as stumbling upon the Surrogate Grandmother's cubicle can be a bit like taking an unexpected field trip to the local nursing home. It's difficult, especially at first, to keep from asking her about the *Titanic* or Prohibition for lack of anything else to say. But over time you will ease up and come to value her emotional availability.

The Surrogate Grandmother is so sweet it almost breaks your heart asking her to work. But it's not as if those expense reports are going to collate themselves, right? So you find yourself dropping by periodically just to leave something on her desk, then sticking around for a half hour or so, chatting, munching on her home-baked oatmeal raisin cookies and looking at old photos. The best thing about her is that she actually listens to you. So you totally fumbled the big sales pitch this morning, pawed the overhead projector like a dumb jock on a first date, and made a mockery of your superiors' wishes? The Surrogate Grandmother doesn't care. She thinks you're wonderful no matter what. She's just happy to have someone to talk to. That superimportant package you neglected to ship overnight? Those files you accidentally deleted? The big client whose lunch invitation you stupidly refused? The Surrogate Grandmother loves you all the same. You are her special little coworker. She says you're precious and calls you "darling." She pats you on the knee and says it's all right. You thank her, smile, and ask after that data entry project you requested. If she had a refrigerator in her cube, the year-end review you just aced would be up there with a magnet.

In some cases, the Surrogate Grandmother isn't even elderly, but middle-aged at most. All that's really required of her is a lack of family, an instinctual need to coddle, and a cardigan sweater draped permanently over the back of her chair. The Surrogate Grandmother leads what is most likely a lonely existence. It is easy to imagine her home life consisting of little more than Celestial Seasonings, reruns of *Matlock,* and the upkeep of a few potted plants or, season permitting, sad and smallish pumpkins. It's best to not think about all that. Obviously, something went drastically wrong with the Surrogate Grandmother's personal life. Perhaps she was once left at the altar or referred to as the "ugly duckling" or voted Least Likely to Find Happiness. Suffice to say that by showering you with affection, the Surrogate Grandmother is probably filling some void in her own life. The whole dynamic is perhaps not quite as selfless as it may seem, but under the present circumstances (i.e., working) it's the best thing you've got. So why ask questions?

In return for her emotional largesse, most coworkers shower the Surrogate Grandmother with their own slew of complimentary comments. Any task she performs, regardless of either difficulty or proficiency, is greeted with a display of superlatives usually reserved for Cy Young Award winners or Nobel laureates. Never before have people tossed around such adjectives as "wonderful," "marvelous," "life saving," "incredible," "miraculous," and "perfect" as they do in the Surrogate Grandmother's presence. Her ability to recall personal detail (your girlfriend's name, your birthday and age, your alma mater) and willingness to express maternal longing may obscure the actual quality of her performance. But who cares? Any idiot can file, but not everyone devotes her free time to running the office's volunteer drive or sends you an e-card when you're feeling down. Next to the paycheck, she's the best thing about your job.

MEMORABLE QUOTES

◆ "What did that mean man say to you?"

◆ "Oh, I wish you could visit a little longer."

◆ "You hang on to that sweet girl. She's a keeper."

THE TEMP

"Uh . . . wha?"

Observing coworkers for future material

Blasting Motörhead at top volume

Binder contains outline for next screenplay

Never actually ties tie, just loosens and pulls over head

Lifts with legs, not back

Career Temp

Intelligent, Creative Temp

The Mule

Well meaning, industrious, and often more intelligent than the salaried employees around him, the Temp is routinely condescended to and taken advantage of. Despite his best intentions, the Temp is marginalized and made to feel inferior whenever possible. Regular employees scoff at the Temp for being paid hourly ("Enjoy your half-hour lunch break") and derive great pleasure flashing HMO cards under his sniffling nose. Though good for a joke or to clean out the supply closet, he is rarely, if ever, made to feel "part of the team." Even Temps on long-term assignment find it difficult to fit in.

Of course, many Temps consider this distinction to rate high among the position's few perks. There's a certain freedom to not caring. Is your job keeping you up at night? Rest assured, the Temp is out getting drunk with college girls while you watch *Temptation Island* alone in bed. Once five p.m. rolls around, all work-related thoughts disappear completely from the Temp's unfettered mind. His day job is a means to an end and nothing more. If rent were free, the Temp wouldn't even be here. See him smiling at you? He's picturing you in the same cube twenty years from now. At which point he'll be long gone. Take advantage of him while you can.

Such freedom comes with a price, however. A Temp must be willing to humor leagues of uncreative, brainwashed automatons. He must act as if the business at hand is somehow interesting, must smile and nod convincingly at the latest banal suggestion thrown his way, must pretend he hasn't been on Instant Messenger all day, must actually learn to tie a tie, and must yield, despite his better judgment, to the commands of every single person in the office. In short, he must stifle his humanity. Still, it's better than working at McDonald's.

Perhaps the greatest perk of temping is the free time. Since any halfway intelligent person (and some monkeys) can perform a full day's schedule of corporate office work in about forty-five minutes, ambitious Temps can really take advantage of their situation. The trick is to make it appear as if your work is much more challenging than it actually is. From a distance, no one can really tell what you're doing at your computer. As long as the boss gets his work by the end of the day (or whenever it's due), a Temp can easily spend seven out of every eight hours working on, say, his first book or latest screenplay. In reality, of course, this extra time is mostly spent sending e-mail, napping, poking through the private files of whomever's computer he's sitting at, or surfing the Internet until his brain hurts.

Due to their professional proximity, the Temp is generally most friendly with the Office Girls. The (largely platonic) attraction goes both ways: to the Temp, Office Girls present a refreshing vision of domestic and professional simplicity seriously lacking from his own circle of theoretically artistic friends and acquaintances. On the flip side, Office Girls, having spent their lives surrounded by thoroughly boring, fratty corporate types, are drawn to the relative mystery of the Temp's purported creativity (signaled by the rumpled copy of *Vanity Fair* open on his desk). Everything is mutual and relative; each sees in the other an illustration of what might have been. Temps are particularly fond of Office Girls with cute European accents.

There is another type of Temp, a type sent to the office in a pinch when no one else is available, a type as useless to the company as they are embarrassing to the agency that sent them. We are talking, of course, of the dreaded Career Temp.

These are the Temps who are relegated to their position due to sheer uselessness. They are sometimes elderly, dress decades out of fashion, and move at a speed closely associated with dripping molasses. These Career Temps rarely make it through the week; exasperated employers have been known to call the agency in order to request, "Next time maybe you could send me somebody with a pulse."

As if the specter of the Career Temp were not discouraging enough, Office Girls (and their supervisors) are often faced with the prospect of receiving (and attempting to train) the single most incompetent Temp of all: the Mule. A mindless and plodding employee, the Mule considers each and every task to represent a challenge on par with splitting the atom. It is usually only a matter of time before the Mule is pulled off the computer and made to lug heavy carts of mail, paper, and supplies around all day. In a last-ditch attempt to wring some productivity out of them, Mules are sometimes assigned to intelligent, creative Temps for guidance, a situation of added responsibility not reflected in the latter's paycheck.

Despite the mindlessness with which most Temp assignments can be mastered, in certain markets it is challenging to find work, even for the most qualified of applicants. It can take months to find placement, especially for those brazen enough to stroll into an agency with a résumé listing a liberal arts major. One surefire way to get a leg up is to have a referral, as better agencies practically require one before they will even speak with a prospective Temp.

The Temp is a necessary, if unfortunate, reality of office life. They can be surly and are terrible at answering phones, but many are quick and efficient workers. Don't be dismayed by the magazines they read at their desks. They don't really work there, anyway.

MEMORABLE QUOTES

◆ "I must have left my tie on the train."

◆ "I think my mouse is broken or something."

◆ "Oh, you wanted to review that letter before I sent it?"

◆ "One day I'll write a book about these people."

PERFORMANCE REVIEW AND DEVELOPMENT REPORT

Employee: <u>The Temptress</u>

> **Only the most significant and important points need to be recorded as a reference for the next review.**

Though an employee of an outside entity (namely, a temporary staffing agency), the Temptress supplies the office with a never-ending stream of underpaid, overworked servants (Temps) and is therefore vital to the continued smooth running of the firm's lower administrative realms.

While her charges must make do without the luxuries of job security or health benefits, the Temptress's ability to secure employment of any kind for people whose primary skill set is highlighted by an admittedly impressive working knowledge of John Cassavetes's career makes her a beloved and admired figure to all who place their fortunes in her hands.

Essentially a corporate pimp, the Temptress acts as a conduit between her clients (the johns) and the Temps (the whores). Though theoretically an advocate for the rights and good treatment of her workers, the Temptress usually sides with the company in event of conflict, as the office represents her own source of livelihood and Temps are nothing if not largely interchangeable.

The Temptress coddles her Temps and makes each feel as if he is the greatest data-entry technician who has ever paired black shoes with a brown belt. She deals most closely with the Office Girls, who are commonly in charge of ordering and scheduling Temps as needed, and regularly showers them with goodies and holiday cards when appropriate. Thus, they consider her the sweetest person ever and just love everything about her, though most couldn't pick her out of a police lineup.

Comments and Recommendations: Ability to coddle and placate underlings suggests possibility of move to middle management, though the cushiness of her present position makes this outcome less than desirable.

PERFORMANCE REVIEW AND DEVELOPMENT REPORT

Employee: The Vulture

> **Only the most significant and important points need to be recorded as a reference for the next review.**

No scrap of communal cake, doughnut, or brownie is safe from the Vulture's unrelenting appetite. He will swoop in to devour the edible remains of all office functions, regardless of whether they are related in any way to his own department. The Vulture spends his day silently stalking the building. He possesses a keen understanding of which hour and on what floor various birthday parties, baby showers, retirement parties, holiday celebrations, and similar soirees are due to take place and can effortlessly attend any number of occasions happening simultaneously.

Despite finishing the last piece, the Vulture never assists with postparty cleanup. Likewise, he engages in no small talk, and his presence is an utter mystery to most participants, who nonetheless allow him to partake of their goods on the possible chance that he is some visiting dignitary, as opposed to the Manager of Internal Communications (i.e., Mass-E-mail Sender) from downstairs.

The Vulture has no need to prepare a lunch from home or purchase one on his break. When there are no parties at which to scavenge, he is quite adept at helping himself to the lovely assortment of brown-bagged lunches littering the shelves of the office refrigerator.

In order to facilitate stealth, the Vulture exhibits the foresight to commandeer some little-used, out-of-the-way meeting room from which he commences his clandestine culinary activity. Victims of the Vulture's prowess attempt to dissuade him by scribbling ineffectual black marker missives on their lunch sacks ("Don't Steal This Lunch!!!!"; "This Is Chuck Hadad's Tuna Fish!!! Leave It Alone!!!!"). The Vulture enjoys reading such correspondence during his lunch hour.

Comments and Recommendations: Money saved on food should facilitate early retirement.

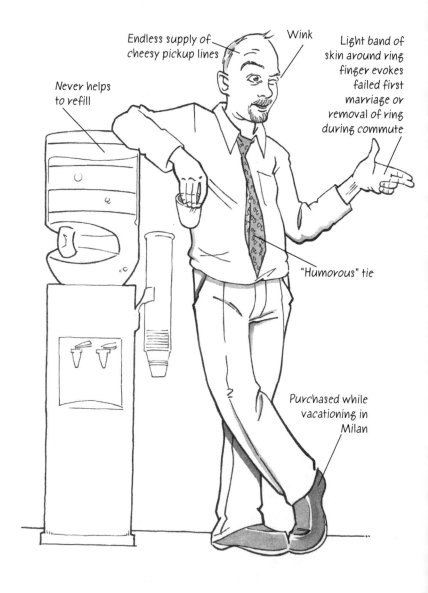

Lock up your secretaries; the Water Cooler Casanova is on the prowl for a new "project." Is he debonair? To a point. Worldly? Negative. Single? Not exactly. Yet the Water Cooler Casanova is the unrivaled philanderer of the workplace. How does he do it? Let us count the ways. The Water Cooler Casanova is a master of female manipulation. He has conquered the aging process, erased all evidence of his pimply adolescence, and subscribed to GQ. This is a man pulling down $40G who wears a $2,000 wristwatch, a man brazen enough to pair blue suspenders with lime green shoes, a man who's cubicle reeks of Tommy cologne. He works out on his lunch break and flirts like he's single.

The Water Cooler Casanova is a man with a tan. So he's pushing forty and graying—that didn't stop him from being spotted last night at two a.m. in the company of the cute new nineteen-year-old Intern. She finds his salt-and-pepper hair charming, and, though she publicly claims repulsion, there she is, all giggles and flushed with wine. Tomorrow morning she'll show up for work bleary-eyed, while the Casanova seems fresh, ready to roll, looking forward to getting his arms around the new revenue-tracking computer system. How does he get away with it? What does his wife think? Those are mysteries of the ages. The Casanova is not bothered by practical considerations.

But wait. This is what the Water Cooler Casanova wants you to think. His ruse is nothing if not well planned. At the end of the day, however, he's painfully aware of his status as a mere cog in the company wheel, a middle manager with no real responsibility of his own, his position the result of a particularly creative HR brainstorm. In an economic crisis, he will be the first person let go. Therefore, the Casanova must be inventive. He must limit his prospective conquests to those women new to the office and therefore unsuspecting of the true nature of his seemingly impressive Associate Vice President of Finance title. That the title carries no real authority is realized only too late by his eager-to-please prey.

In keeping with his status as master manipulator, the Water Cooler Casanova woos the ladies by showering them with extra attention of a seemingly professional nature. Remember, these are young women new to the office. They have yet to establish their own corporate footing and are eager to get ahead. Many are placed under direct supervision of the Water Cooler Casanova, who wastes no time in granting those with "lots of potential" (if you get his meaning) opportunities a less attractive Intern would kill for. Particularly smarmy is his habit of assigning these women to projects requiring frequent after-hours meetings in order to get them in his clutches. This is all proposed professionally enough, the Casanova practically purring, "It will be a really great experience for you." Five weeks later, there's a scene in the parking lot: he's fuming, her eyes are misty, several people notice but none warn the cute blonde hired yesterday.

The Water Cooler Casanova carries himself as if he's the office's Big Man on Campus. If the company offered letter varsity jackets, he'd wear one. As it is, he tends to favor cool designer businesswear much of the week, then really lets lose on Casual Friday, when he whips out his Diesel jeans. He's got a certain swagger, a fake and leering smile, a veritable sparkle in his eye. He's very hands on, likes to get in there real close when he's talking to you. You can hear him coming from three cubes away, but just try turning up the volume on your headphones to discourage him. If he wants to chat, he's gonna chitchat. Have your football pool sheet filled out and ready to go. Though he'd never admit it, the Water Cooler Casanova would kill for a seasonal departmental pep rally.

Coworkers tend to regard the Casanova with a certain level of detached wonder. Many consider him an annoying presence, though he's not quite obnoxious enough to inspire outright hatred. Lonely, quiet guys around the office admire and envy his luck with the ladies. Aging women secretly thrill at his incredibly manipulative practice of extending to them the gift of his flirtations. Most, however, simply marvel that he's yet to be fired for sexual harassment. The Water Cooler Casanova carries on affair after affair right under the boss's watchful eye! And what about his victims? Their failure to report him absolutely boggles the mind. The Water Cooler Casanova single-handedly sets the women's movement back thirty years on a near weekly basis.

MEMORABLE QUOTES

◆ "Have you ever fished off the company pier?"

◆ "Baby, you put the 'ass' back in 'assistant.'"

◆ "Why don't we discuss this project after work, say, at my place?"

THE WEB DESIGN TEAM

At high risk for sunburn during Burning Man

Only flat-screen monitor in the office

Immune to dress code

Claims to be a gift from never-seen girlfriend

Finished Baldur's Gate 2 on company time

Originally purchased for use in freshman dorm shower

Have you ever wished you could stroll into the office around noon, wearing jeans, sandals, and a baseball cap (dress code be damned)? Or maybe you'd like to play video games at your desk? Does interacting with coworkers strike you as an unnecessary nuisance? Would you like to come and go as you please without fear of reprisal? Looking to turn your social anxiety disorder into a career? What if you could do all this and still make more money than everyone else in the office? Well, welcome to the wonderful world of Web design!

Meet the Web Design Team. These are people who passionately believe in the value of their own creativity yet lack the conviction to give up their corporate paycheck. All of their collective slacking (the lax dress code, the abnormal hours, etc.) is little more than a feeble attempt to lend some aspect of the bohemian aesthetic to their ultraconservative, financially rewarding corporate lifestyle. Members of the Web Design Team want everyone to know how "different" and "artistic" they are. They're free thinkers! They wear hemp! They're white, but they like hip-hop (check out that Rawkus bag)! They're like the cast of *Moulin Rouge*! Ah, but there they are, obsessing over the latest tally of their 401(k) accounts.

Granted, now that most corporations have finally figured out that any fifth-grader can create and maintain a Web site, members of the Web Design Team are not compensated quite as lucratively (or ludicrously) as they were just a few years prior (when clearing $100,000 for basically hanging out all day was the norm), but still the position carries with it an earning potential available only to those fortunate enough to bill on a freelance basis. As subcontractors, the Web Design Team is paid on a "for work" basis, the standards of which they determine themselves. This is economic chicanery on a level you can only dream of.

In today's corporate climate, many companies choose to contract Web work out to an off-site entity. However, enough Teams are still employed on-site to make them an office fixture. Though fully integrated into office culture, the Web Design Team exists on a frontier well removed from other workers (usually in a cluster of out-of-the-way workstations abandoned during rounds of heavy layoffs). They sit and travel in packs, and the Team as a whole is overwhelmingly young (nineteen to twenty-three) and male. Most decorate their workstations in a near identical manner: photographs of (possibly fictional) girlfriends, certificate of completion from the Devry Institute of Technology (or other pseudo institutes of higher learning), super badass computer (despite the fact that they could perform the majority of their duties on a Commodore 64), and kitschy Web site–related tchotchkes (coffee mug from www.hotornot.com, Intel stress ball, Kozmo.com, bicycle helmet, etc.).

When not actually coding or designing (which is often), the Team enjoys discussing video game action in realistic, true-to-life terms and debating the merits of various electronica musical subgenres (acid house vs. trance, for example). The Web Design Team is incredibly pop culture savvy, especially in geek terms, and it is this characteristic that most readily separates them from the more bookish IT Guy.

The Web Design Team is actually made up of two distinct personalities. Perhaps most visible is the Graphic Designer, an artsy prima donna who dabbled in collage before realizing there's no money in it. In order to overcome a nasty case of postgraduate uselessness, the Graphic Designer wisely bought a few books and taught himself Photoshop, Illustrator, and a bit of basic HTML (it's that simple!). The second member of the Team is the Web Developer. This is the true techie, a man largely indistinguishable from the Condescending IT Guy. However, he exists higher up the geek food chain than a standard-issue Network Administrator, mostly due to the fact that, instead of playing technological babysitter to the office drones, he codes all the back-end functions of the Web site itself (basically making all the elements created by the Graphic Designer "work"). The Web Developer possesses literally no social skills. None.

MEMORABLE QUOTES

◆ "ByteArray objects cannot be converted to strings. Obviously."

◆ "Well, if you must know, the specifics of my dating history can be found in the archives of my live journal."

◆ "Oh, shit . . . I think I left my I-Pod in the Jetta."

Orbiting the boss like Jupiter's moons, Yes Men are drawn to their superior by a strong gravitational attraction often referred to as "brown-nosing" or "ass-kissing." However, unlike the official office Brown Noser, the Yes Men have already ascended to positions of authority (the only remaining promotional option is the boss's job itself, and they've got no chance of landing that), and so their sycophantic nature speaks more to a personal need to feel appreciated than a professional desire to get ahead. The Yes Men exist for no other reason than to pledge their unwavering support to the boss.

Being a Yes Man can be quite precarious. Since their success is tied directly to that of the current regime, Yes Men sometimes ride the boss's coattails down the corporate ladder as fast as they rode them up. If the boss is forced out or retires, they are left with little ground to cling to and are usually shown the door soon after (to the delight of the office at large). However, as much as you might like to imagine the Yes Men living out the remainder of their days at some Dust Bowl–era work camp, most manage to land at other corporations, where their lapdoglike servitude is highly appreciated by the resident man in power.

Yes Men travel in packs of three to six and dress in a style identical to the boss's favorite fashions. Since they march in unison, it is easy to hear them approaching from a distance. By placing your ear to the tiled floor of the restroom, it is possible to pick up the quick staccato rhythm of their footsteps (as well as their orchestrated group laughter) from even the most remote corners of the office. You should take care to avoid them for several reasons: first, for fear of physical injury (they break for no one and will not hesitate to stomp all over your cheap brown loafers), second, they have been known to greet those outside their circle with incredibly patronizing commentary ("So, how's the split-level working out?"), and third, if you're unlucky enough to be employed on an administrative level, the Yes Men will no doubt dispatch you on some unbelievably unnecessary errand simply because they can. Your goal is to do as little work as possible, right? So stay away from these guys.

The Yes Men may have some good ideas of their own, but they will never, ever present them. They wait until the boss has made his feelings known, then concur with great vigor. Some Yes Men have experienced actual whiplash from nodding their heads in agreement, not that this has any effect on their spinelessness. Yes Men flip-flop like fish out of water and are less logical than the employee handbook. With any change of heart on the boss's part, they quickly abandon their former position to better align themselves with his new one. This is done in a spirit of intense rivalry; each Yes Man ardently strives to be the first to voice his staunch support for the boss's latest brainstorm. There is no sense of friendship or camaraderie within their ranks. Those slow on the uptake (or even slightly hesitant to abandon personal integrity) can take days to recover emotionally; shunned Yes Men regularly pass the late-evening hours poring over old favorable year-end reviews, sobbing into bottles of low carb beer, and repolishing their wing tips.

As mentioned above, Yes Men have already managed to ascend the corporate ladder through years of successful brownnosing and golf playing. So why do they continue to jockey for position? Why is the conference table seat directly to the boss's right more hotly contested than the remaining musical chair at a six-year-old's birthday party? Well, if you've ever had the unfortunate experience of spending any real time with them (awkward small talk at the company's Bring Your Daughter to Work Day, perhaps), it's obvious that these guys weren't the ones dating the cheerleaders in high school. The Yes Men were probably good at math and maybe played a little tennis to satisfy some phys ed requirement, but if there's an adjective that might best have described them, it wouldn't be "cool." So this is their big chance. The boss is, after all, the Big Man on Campus, the guy who calls the shots and sleeps with any secretary who strikes his fancy, the one man everybody else secretly wishes he could be. The Yes Men are finally members of the right clique. They fit in, they're popular, they flirt with all the right Receptionists, and all it cost them was their dignity.

MEMORABLE QUOTES

◆ "That's the best idea I've ever heard, sir. Better than the zipper."

◆ "Well, I would agree. Strike that. I would *wholeheartedly* agree."

◆ "Not only is your recommendation brilliant, but I would propose that it's genius as well."

◆ "Of course I can come in on Saturday. Let me just cancel these twentieth-anniversary plans."

ACKNOWLEDGMENTS

Nobody deconstructs the drudgery of his surroundings quite like Chuck Hadad, a man brazen enough to e-mail me actual porn to illustrate the Porno Purveyor's handiwork and the mastermind behind the Water Cooler Casanova entry, among others. Nancy Barbosa took time out from her fairy-tale life in Notting Hill to weigh in with a stream of wonderfully condescending remarks. Aside from being the musical genius behind Metallic Pea, Jim Marchese leapt at any opportunity to put his own work aside and do mine for me. Jackie Endriss and Chris Naughton both outdid themselves in supplying me with the latest in business-speak and the minutiae of corporate culture. My long-lost friend Kamila Fix came out of nowhere to clue me in on a variety of workplace detail unknown to the common temp. Thank God she married a former consultant. Amy De-Cicco, though far removed from corporate life (fortunately for her), spent three solid months listening to me whine about this project. Michael Tully was instrumental in commiserating about our time spent slaving together in midtown, while Beth Datlowe should score huge brownie points with her boss (my editor) for sharing her collected thoughts on workplace oddities. Also, I'd be remiss if I didn't mention that Kyle Bernstein is perhaps the funniest, crotchetiest person I've ever gone to Hebrew school with.

Whew. The list goes on. My sister, Stefanie Aiello, was always there in a pinch, as were Dorothy Robinson, Jeremy Schiffer, Patrick O'Grady, Edward Hadad, Matt Roberts, Pam Oakman, Judi DeCicco, David Winn, my parents (Joseph and Linda Aiello), Bill Griffith, Matthew Fix, Shannon Maydick, Michelle Radwanski, Kathy Lendle, Regan Whitehead, Michelle Stark, Miriam Sokolowski, Kathleen Kenny, and Marina Rozanova.

Becky Cole possesses all the qualities anyone could wish for in an editor, including impeccable grammar (particularly a deft mastery of the split infinitive), and a flexible understanding of the term "due date." I sincerely hope that she continues to present me with new book ideas just as I've run out of money.

Despite his foolhardy insistence on rooting for the New York Mets, the recently retired Mike Harriot's good taste, unflagging enthusiasm, and ability to pay for beer will be sorely missed. Though I intend to persuade him to open a single-client agency à la Jerry Maguire (Mike, you had me at "I'll sign you"), I also wish him the best of luck in his new career. P.S. Go Phillies.

ABOUT THE AUTHOR AND ILLUSTRATOR

JOSH AIELLO (right) owns two pairs of Dockers (both khaki) and can type thirty-five words per minute. He has lent his word-processing expertise to *Men's Health* magazine, the National Academy of Television Arts and Sciences, and Fleet Bank, among others. In addition to his data-entry prowess and knack for alphabetical filing, Josh excels at drinking coffee and has been known to read the *New York Times Magazine* with one hand while processing 401(k) rollover requests with the other. Josh is the author of *A Field Guide to the Urban Hipster*, and, according to a recently administered Caliper Profile Evaluation, "it could be important to provide him with regular positive feedback and ego-boosts."

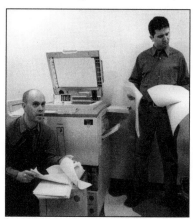

MATTHEW SHULTZ is a native Michigander living in Brooklyn. He has spent thousands of hours in the cubes, busily working for work's own sake, like in the WPA or Soviet Russia. He met Josh Aiello while the two were briefly toiling under the same wagemaster. Matthew's countless awards and accolades (including two consecutive "Teller of the Month" honors at Commerce Bank in St. Louis) show how beloved he is by his employers, none of whom look anything like any of the drawings in this book.